The Freshwater Angler™

WALLEYE
Patterns & Presentations

•••••••••••••••••

How to Catch Trophy Fish in Lakes, Rivers and Reservoirs

CREATIVE
PUBLISHING
international

MINNETONKA, MINNESOTA

www.howtobookstore.com

CREDITS

Creative Publishing international, Inc.
5900 Green Oak Drive
Minnetonka, MN 55343
1-800-328-3895
www.howtobookstore.com

President/CEO: David D. Murphy
Vice President/Editorial: Patricia K. Jacobsen
Vice President/Retail Sales & Marketing: Richard M. Miller

WALLEYE PATTERNS & PRESENTATIONS

Executive Editor, Outdoor Group: Don Oster
Editorial Director: David R. Maas
Managing Editor: Jill Anderson
Editor: Steven Hauge
Creative Director: Brad Springer
Senior Art Director: David W. Schelitzche
Art Director: Joe Fahey
Photo Researcher: Angela Hartwell
Director, Production Services: Kim Gerber
Production Manager: Helga Thielen
Production Staff: Stephanie Barakos, Laura Hokkanen

Back Cover Photo of Gary Roach: Northland Fishing Tackle

Contributing Photographer:
Bill Lindner Photography
  www.blpstudio.com
  ©Bill Lindner Photography: pp. 151, 154-155

Contributing Illustrator:
Joseph R. Tomelleri
  www.americanfishes.com
  ©Joseph R. Tomelleri: pp. 28-29, 30-31

Printed on American paper by: R. R. Donnelley & Sons Co.
10 9 8 7 6 5 4 3 2 1

ISBN 0-86573-130-6

CONTENTS

For DECADES, WALLEYES HAVE BEEN THE FAVORITE OF FRESHWATER ANGLERS THROUGHOUT MOST OF THE NORTHERN STATES AND CANADA. And the walleye's popularity has spread to other parts of the country as a result of widespread stocking in southern and western states.

It is not surprising that the walleye is held in such high regard throughout North America. Its finicky feeding habits can frustrate even the most patient, expert anglers, so there is a feeling of accomplishment when a successful pattern is found, resulting in a good catch. Another reason for the walleye's popularity is its well-deserved reputation as table fare—it's simply one of the best-eating freshwater fish.

The purpose of this book is to help you catch walleyes more consistently in a variety of conditions. Anyone can catch biters; limits can be easy when 'eyes go on a feeding binge. However, much of the time they seem to hide and refuse to feed, and it takes a great deal of knowledge, skill and perseverance to find and catch them. This book will show you the most advanced techniques and equipment and further your understanding of the behavior of this sometimes perplexing species.

The first chapter, "Walleye-Fishing Equipment," helps you select the proper type of equipment for your local fishing conditions. It includes everything from rods and reels to sophisticated electronic devices that will serve as your eyes under the water, helping you to identify likely fish-producing places.

"Understanding the Walleye" is the most complete treatise on walleye behavior in print today and includes contributions by noted expert walleye biologists from across North America. You'll gain a better understanding of walleye behavior and learn where to find walleyes in each season. Armed with this information, you'll be ready to develop your own successful walleye-fishing strategies.

"Basic Walleye-Fishing Techniques" shows you how to locate good walleye water and how to recognize the places likely to hold walleyes. Once you've located good walleye-holding structure, you'll see all-important boat-control techniques to work it properly. You'll also learn the live-bait and artificial-lure techniques used to catch walleyes consistently. This chapter teaches you how to detect strikes and set the hook when using a slip-sinker rig, how to present a jig, and how to master lesser-known techniques like slip-bobber fishing.

The final chapter, "Techniques for Special Situations," goes beyond the basics of walleye fishing. You'll learn how to catch walleyes buried in dense weeds, heavy timber or brush. And you'll find out how experts cope with tough fishing conditions like ultra-clear water, the spawning season and the days following a cold front.

The clearly written text and spectacular color photographs and illustrations in this book provide you with the knowledge and techniques used by North America's top walleye-fishing experts. Whether you're a beginner or an expert, *Walleye Patterns & Presentations* will greatly improve your walleye catches.

1

WALLEYE-FISHING
EQUIPMENT

Rods, Reels & Line
for Walleye Fishing

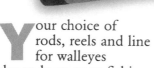

Your choice of rods, reels and line for walleyes depends on your fishing technique. Anglers who regularly use several techniques during a day of fishing often carry three or four rod-and-reel outfits, each set up with different lures or live-bait rigs.

The following recommendations will help you choose the rods, reels and line best suited to your style of fishing.

RODS. For casting and trolling with lures and live-bait rigs weighing from 1/4 to 5/8 ounce, select a 6-foot, medium-power, fast-action spinning rod (above). This rod is the best choice for general-purpose walleye fishing.

For casting small jigs, and other lures and rigs weighing from 1/16 to 1/8 ounce, select a 6- to 6 1/2-foot, light-power, fast-action spinning rod. This rod flexes easily on the backcast, so it works well for propelling light lures and baits.

Casting and trolling with large deep-diving crankbaits and live-bait rigs weighing more than 1/2 ounce is easiest with a 6- to 6 1/2-foot, medium-power, fast-action bait-casting rod. Because this rod has more backbone than most spinning rods, it is better suited to heavier lures and rigs.

If you fish mainly with live bait, a 6 1/2- to 7 1/2-foot light-power, medium-action spinning rod is a better choice than a short, stiffer rod. A light-power rod flexes easily, so a walleye would feel little resistance should it shake its head or make some other unexpected move after it picks up the bait. A medium-power rod would not flex as much, so the

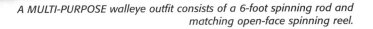

A MULTI-PURPOSE walleye outfit consists of a 6-foot spinning rod and matching open-face spinning reel.

walleye would feel more resistance and probably drop the bait. A long, flexible rod also casts live bait better than a stiffer rod. Because the rod absorbs most of the snap, the bait is less likely to fly off the hook.

Walleyes are notoriously soft biters. As a result, sensitivity should be a major consideration in choosing a walleye rod. Notice that most of the recommended rods have a fast action; slower-action rods are not as sensitive. Most serious walleye fishermen prefer graphite rods because they transmit vibrations better than fiberglass rods.

> **QUICK TIP:** Rod blanks that extend completely through the handle have better sensitivity than those that extend only partway through. If the blank does not extend completely through, the handle material will dampen the vibrations before they reach your hand.

Other features that improve a rod's ability to transmit vibrations include a blank that extends all the way through the rod handle; one-piece construction; and lightweight, single-foot guides. Ferrules and double-foot guides add weight and tend to restrict the rod's action.

REELS. For good sensitivity and casting performance, your reel must balance with your rod. Check the lure- and line-weight recommendations on both your rod and reel to make sure that they match. For example, if you attempt to use a reel intended for 12- to 20-pound line with a rod designed for 4- to 8-pound line, the outfit will be butt-heavy. Too much weight on the butt end makes casting difficult because it interferes with your wrist snap. And the weight dampens the sensation from a subtle bite.

When selecting a spinning reel, look for the following features:

•*Drag location.* Rear drags are easy to adjust when playing fish because you do not have to reach in front of the spool. Front drags are generally smoother, but smoothness is not a major consideration in walleye fishing because the fish generally do not make long runs.

•*A bail with strong spring tension.* If the bail does not close all the way, the line will ride on the bail itself rather than on the roller. When you attempt to set the hook, the bail will open enough to let line come off the spool. Some of the best spinning reels have a spring on each end of the bail.

•*A free-turning bail roller.* The roller must turn when the line passes over it. If it does not, heat and abrasion will damage the line and may wear a groove in the roller.

•*Interchangeable spools.* These spools snap into the reel, enabling you to quickly change to a different weight or type of line, or to replace a half-empty spool with a full one.

•*Spool size.* A spinning-reel spool should be large enough to prevent the line from developing memory, which causes it to come off in tight coils. The diameter of a spinning-reel spool should be at least $1\frac{1}{2}$ inches for 6-pound mono, $1\frac{7}{8}$ inches for 10-pound mono.

QUICK TIP: Use baitcasting reels whenever you cast or troll with crankbaits. The low gear ratio is perfect for cranking in these hard-pulling lures.

In selecting a baitcasting reel, the most important feature is backlash resistance. Good baitcasting reels have some type of magnetic or centrifugal brake system to keep backlashing to a minimum. A high gear ratio is not a requirement for walleye fishing because fast retrieves are seldom needed. A gear ratio of 4:1 is usually adequate. Some baitcasting reels also come with interchangeable line spools.

Although most experienced walleye fishermen frown on spin-casting gear, it remains a favorite among many anglers. If you purchase a spin-cast reel, make sure it has a smooth drag and a reliable line-pickup mechanism. Unless the line is taut, the mechanism on a cheap spin-cast reel often fails to pick up the line when you turn the handle.

LINE. Walleyes can be very line shy, especially in clear water. To keep line visibility to a minimum, use clear monofilament or mono tinted to match the color of the water. In low-clarity water, line color generally makes little difference.

QUICK TIP: When fishing in rocks or other heavy cover, check your line often for abrasions. It's not uncommon to have to retie several times an hour.

Regardless of water clarity, it pays to use the lightest, limpest, lowest-diameter line that suits the conditions. Line with these characteristics flows off the spool more easily than heavier, stiffer or thicker line. As a result, you can cast farther and feed line more easily when a walleye runs with your bait. And wobbling lures can move more freely.

Unless you are fishing in heavy cover, you will seldom need monofilament heavier than 8-pound test. When fishing in rocks, brush or dense weeds, you may have to sacrifice limpness for stiffer, more abrasion-resistant line.

TIPS ON CARING FOR RODS, REELS AND LINE

•*Lubricate* each side of the bail assembly with a spray-type lubricant to prevent binding. Use light machine oil on the handle and shaft, then remove the housing cover and spread a few drops on the gears.

•*Pull* a piece of nylon stocking through the guides to check for cracks or grooves that could fray your line. The nylon will snag on rough spots.

•*Clean* the cork handles of your walleye rods by lightly rubbing them with fine sandpaper.

•*Straighten* twisted line by removing any hardware, then letting the line out behind your boat. Keep your boat moving at a fast trolling speed, and continue to pull off line until your spool is about half full. After a few minutes of trolling, your line will be free of twists.

Boats, Motors & Accessories

Walleye anglers who do most of their fishing on big water prefer 16- to 18-foot boats with wide, deep semi-V hulls. A large outboard, usually 40 to 115 hp, makes it possible to reach shore quickly should a storm blow up. On the Great Lakes, walleye fishermen often use boats 25 to 30 feet long for safety.

A 14-foot semi-V with a 10- to 15-hp motor is adequate for smaller waters, and has probably accounted for more walleyes than any other type of rig.

Flat-bottom or other low-profile designs work well on small to medium-sized rivers and lakes, but are not a good choice on waters subject to heavy wave action. Semi-V hulls are drier and safer. They have high sides and are designed to slice through the waves.

Most walleye fishermen prefer boats with aluminum hulls because they are lighter, more durable and less expensive than those with fiberglass hulls. But fiberglass hulls are quieter and not as likely to develop leaks. Because they ride lower in the water, they are less affected by the wind, so the boat is much easier to control.

Walleye fishing usually demands a slow presentation, so your outboard motor should be capable of trolling at a very low speed. Slow trolling is seldom a problem with motors under 25 hp. But larger motors may not run smoothly at low

speed. Generally, a motor with three or four cylinders will troll more smoothly than one with two cylinders.

What accessories you need on your boat depends on your style of fishing and how seriously you wish to pursue the sport. Most tournament walleye pros have boats rigged with practically every accessory available. A casual walleye angler obviously would not need such an elaborate rig. A 14-foot aluminum semi-V with a 15-hp motor can be rigged with the equipment necessary for most situations.

Following are some of the more important accessories and their functions:

•*A tiller handle* for precise boat control. A motor with a tiller is a better choice than one controlled by a steering wheel, especially for backtrolling. With a tiller, you can steer and operate the throttle with one hand, leaving the other hand free for fishing.

•*An electric starter* for outboards larger than 25 hp. Smaller outboards can easily be started with a pull cord. If possible, select a motor with an alternator so that you do not have to recharge your starter battery.

•*A flasher* to indicate depth, fish location and bottom type. Anglers who use bow-mounted trolling motors often have a flasher in the front of the boat as well as one in the rear.

•*A liquid-crystal depth finder* to provide detailed information on fish location and bottom type.

•*A transom-mounted electric motor* for backtrolling more slowly and quietly than you could with an outboard. An electric also saves gasoline, and you do not have to inhale any fumes.

•*A bow-mounted electric motor with foot controls* for motoring while casting lures or bait rigs. Foot controls allow you to keep your hands free.

•*A GPS navigator* for returning to fishing spots on large bodies of water. This device calculates the exact latitude and longitude of the spot where you are fishing based on satellite signals. When you wish to return to that spot, the device gives you steering instructions and the distance to go before reaching the spot.

•*A surface-temperature gauge* for locating areas with favorable water temperatures. This device is most valuable in spring, when most of the fish are in the shallows. Later, surface temperature becomes less important because the walleyes have moved deeper.

•*Pedestal or clamp-on seats* to provide back support and make your fishing more comfortable.

•*A lockable rod-storage compartment.*

•*Lockable compartments* for storing other gear.

•*An aerated live well* for keeping fish and live bait.

•*An electric bilge pump* for removing water from the bottom of the boat.

•*A compass* to aid in navigation.

•*Power trim* for adjusting the angle of your motor to suit the load. Power trim also enables you to tilt your motor up to move through shallow water and to slow your back-trolling speed.

•*A marine battery* for starting your outboard and operating a flasher, graph, aerator, bilge pump and other low-draw accessories. A marine battery is better for starting than a deep-cycle battery because it has more cold-cranking power. Do not use an automotive battery, because the plates are not designed to withstand pounding from waves.

•*Deep-cycle batteries* for high-draw accessories like trolling motors. These batteries can be drawn down and recharged many more times than marine batteries.

•*A stainless-steel propeller* for large outboards. A stainless-steel prop does not flex as much as an aluminum prop, so it has more torque. And it is much less likely to be damaged by hitting rocks.

•*Splash guards* to prevent water from sloshing over the transom when backtrolling in rough water.

•*A Navy-style anchor* and a rope at least three times as long as the deepest water you normally fish. Many anglers use a second anchor to prevent the stern from swinging. A 15-pound anchor is usually adequate for a boat of 15 feet or less, but you may need a 25-pound anchor to hold an 18-foot boat.

Fishing Electronics

I f you asked a successful walleye angler to name his single most important piece of walleye-fishing equipment, he would say a depth finder. Without one, finding walleyes is nothing more than guesswork. What's the second most important? On large bodies of water, where

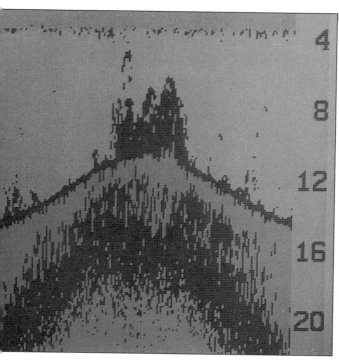

LIQUID-CRYSTAL RECORDERS display the sonar signal on a screen made up of tiny squares, or pixels. For good resolution, the vertical pixel count should be at least 128. Some LCRs can be linked to GPS modules, which turn the sonar device into a GPS navigation instrument.

finding the spot on the spot is difficult at best, the same angler would say his GPS (Global Positioning System) navigational system.

Before the age of electronic fishing, anglers had only a vague idea of water depth and bottom contour. And if they found a hot walleye spot on a big lake or reservoir, they would have to be lucky to find it a second time.

Modern walleye anglers rely on their depth finders to check depth, to find structure and to find fish on that structure. GPS systems allow anglers to return to a specific location time after time, even after dark or in a thick fog.

SONAR DEVICES. Commonly called depth finders or fish locators, sonar devices come in three basic types: liquid-crystal recorders (LCRs), video graphs and flashers.

All sonar devices operate on the same principle. The transducer, which can be attached to the boat's hull, transom or trolling motor, sends sound waves to the bottom, and the returning echos are recorded on a screen or, in the case of a flasher, displayed instantly on a dial. The screen or dial displays the bottom and any other objects above it, such as fish or weeds. With a little experience, the operator can also learn to distinguish different bottom types.

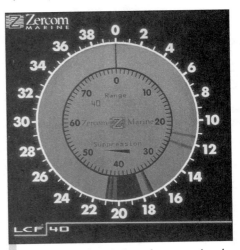

FLASHERS (above) show the sonar signal on a calibrated dial or bar display. Unlike other sonar devices, flashers give you an instantaneous readout of targets, even at speeds over 60 mph. For this reason, flashers are the favorite sonar device for many expert fishermen.

VIDEO GRAPHS display the sonar signal on a cathode-ray tube, much like a television set. Videos are bulky, but give you better resolution than an LCR. Some video graphs have a color display, with different colors representing different-sized targets.

17

When selecting a sonar unit, consider the cone angle of the transducer, which determines how much of the bottom the sonar signal covers. A narrow cone (20 degrees or less) is best for detecting bottom-hugging walleyes because it has a thinner "blind spot" (page 19) than a wide-cone transducer. A wider cone is better for vertically jigging or downrigger trolling for suspended fish, because you can monitor a larger area and see the depth of your lure or cannonball.

> QUICK TIP: Mount a transducer to the bottom of a bow-mounted trolling motor. This placement makes it easy for you to easily fish along weedlines and breaklines.

Understanding "Hook Size" on a Graph

Many fishermen think a big hook on their LCR or video means a big fish. It could be, but it could also mean a small fish. Here's why.

Suppose two fish of equal size swim underneath your stationary boat. The first fish (number 1 in example A, opposite page), is only a few feet down, where the cone is narrow. As a result, it passes through the cone quickly and makes only a short mark. The second fish (2) swims near the bottom, where the cone is wide. It spends more time in the cone, and consequently makes a much longer mark.

Here's another example: You're drifting or slow-trolling and pass over a perch (number 3 in example B) that is motionless or swimming slowly with the boat. It makes a long mark because it stays in the cone until the boat moves away. Then a good-sized walleye (4) swims rapidly through the cone. It makes a shorter mark because it passes through the cone more quickly.

A more reliable indicator of fish size than arc length is arc thickness. The thickness depends on the strength of the reflected signal. And big fish reflect a much stronger signal than do little fish.

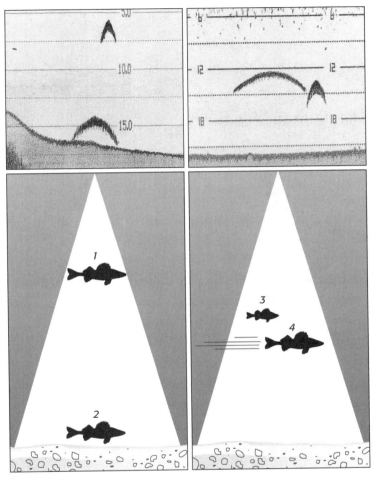

Example A   Example B

Understanding a Depth Finder's Blind Spot

It's a mistake to fish only where you "see" fish with your flasher, LCR or video. These devices have a blind spot or "dead zone" — an area in the sound cone where a depth finder cannot display any targets. As the illustration on page 20 shows, the dead zone is thickest at the edge of the

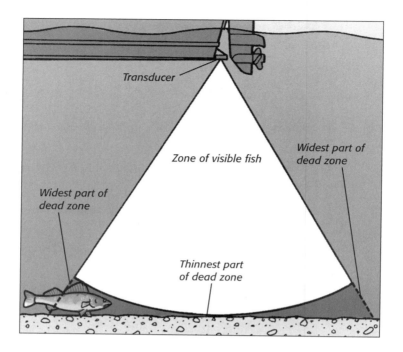

Transducer

Zone of visible fish

Widest part of
dead zone

Widest part of
dead zone

Thinnest part
of dead zone

cone and thinnest directly beneath the transducer. If walleyes are in this zone, you won't see them.

The thickness of the blind spot directly beneath the transducer is determined by your sonar device's target separation, which is the depth finder's ability to distinguish and display targets that are close together vertically. These targets could be fish, weeds or the bottom.

For example, if your sonar device has a target separation of 3 inches, and two small walleye swim through the sound cone one on top of the other, the locator will display them as a single target. However, if the two fish separate so one is swimming 4 inches higher than the other, the sonar will display them as two targets. In other words, if your sonar has a target separation of 3 inches, the blind spot directly beneath the transducer is 3 inches thick.

To understand why the blind spot is thickest at the edge of the cone, you must be familiar with how a sonar device displays the depth. For example, suppose the verticle distance from your transducer to the bottom measures 15 feet.

The only objects that are seen on the locator's screen are those that are less than 15 feet away from the transducer (opposite page, Zone of visible fish). But a fish just off the bottom and on the edge of the cone is more than 15 feet away from the transducer and lost in the blind spot.

You can't eliminate the blind spot, but you can gain a better understanding of what's happening beneath the boat by determining how thick the zone for your depth finder really is. Drop a jig to the bottom. Lower the rod tip to the water and reel in any slack. Lift the rod tip until the jig appears on the depth finder, and note the distance between the water and rod tip. That distance is the thickness of your blind spot in that particular part of the sound cone and depth of water.

Global Positioning Systems

These units, simply called GPS, are a dream for big-water fishermen. This navigational system has made it possible for walleye anglers to return to a particular piece of structure, time and time again.

GPS systems operate on signals received from U.S. military satellites.

FULL-SIZE GPS UNITS have a separate antenna, or module, that receives the satellite signals. They are powered by the boat's 12-volt electrical system. They have a large, easy-to-read screen. Combination units bring together the full-size GPS navigational system and a liquid-crystal depth finder into one compact unit. Handheld GPS units (right) are powered by an internal battery and have a built-in antenna, so they are portable. They have the same features as a full-size GPS unit, but the screen is much smaller.

Because of this, the system can be used anywhere walleyes are found on earth.

Many anglers are intimidated by the complexity of these systems, so they are hesitant to purchase one. One reason GPS systems seem so complex is that they have many advanced features that the average angler may never use. Most walleye fishermen simply want to mark the location of a particular waypoint, such as a good fishing spot or a boat landing, so they can find it again later. The procedure for doing that is quite simple.

After you use your navigation unit for awhile and become comfortable with it, you can begin experimenting with some of the more complex features, such as setting up a navigation route that leads you to a series of waypoints.

GPS has become very popular because it is easy to operate. You do not have to program the unit to select certain signals, as you did with other navigational systems. And it is more reliable, because it is not affected by weather. Another advantage: GPS units process navigation data very rapidly, usually within a second or two. Because the screen is updated so fast, there is less chance for steering error.

Other Walleye-
Fishing Equipment

You do not need all of the equipment discussed on these pages to catch walleyes. Many of the items are merely conveniences, but others will definitely help you catch more fish.

Drift socks slow your drift on a windy day, so you can present your bait at a speed attractive to walleyes. Some models have a cord you can pull to adjust the bag capacity, regulating your speed.

The value of many of these items depends on the type of fishing you do. For example, if you fish on a tiny lake, a GPS would be of little use. But it would be an invaluable aid on a large body of water where returning to a productive spot may be difficult, especially at night or in foggy weather.

It pays to carry a well-equipped tool kit stocked with extra spark plugs, shear pins and fuses in case of an equipment breakdown. Some anglers even carry an extra propeller and gas hose. A pair of longnose pliers makes it easier to unhook fish and helps you avoid cutting your fingers on sharp teeth and gill covers.

If you have a storage compartment in your boat, stash a waterproof bag containing a set of raingear and a pair of rubber boots in case of foul weather. Keep your hooks and other terminal tackle in a small watertight plastic box with compartments for each item. A first-aid kit is also a good item to keep on board.

Anyone who operates a fishing boat must be aware of federal, state and provincial regulations concerning life preservers, fire extinguishers, horns and other safety equipment.

Floating markers (below) give you a reference point so you can thoroughly work a piece of structure. And when you catch a walleye, you can pinpoint the spot and possibly catch several more from the same area.

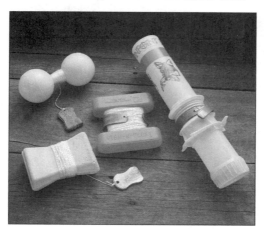

Spotlights make it possible to see walleyes in shallow water after dark. You can easily identify the fish because of their glowing eyes. Although the light spooks the fish, you can return later and catch them.

Flasher hoods help you read the signal in bright sunlight. You can buy a hood for most popular models or make your own by shaping a piece of sheet metal to fit your unit. Most flasher hoods are attached by the thumbscrews on the sides.

Swivel mounts enable you to rotate your flasher or liquid crystal for better visibility and to remove it from the boat quickly. Some models snap together to hold the unit in place; others are locked into position by turning a screw at the base.

Hook files enable you to keep a needle-sharp point on lure and live-bait hooks. Test the sharpness of a hook by sliding the point over your thumbnail. If the point slides easily without catching, the hook is too dull.

Coolers work well for keeping fish and bait in hot weather. Warm water makes it difficult to keep walleyes alive on a stringer or in a live well. And nightcrawlers or leeches may not survive a whole day if exposed to the sun.

Tackle Tamers (right) are ideal for storing spinner rigs. Insert the hook through the eyelet and wind the leader on snugly. Use the Velcro® tab to secure the free end to prevent the rig from coming loose and tangling.

Flow-through bait buckets keep baitfish lively, but only if the surface water is cool. If the water is too warm, place the bucket in a cooler or keep bait in an insulated container with ice.

2

UNDERSTANDING THE
WALLEYE

Walleye Basics

The elusive nature of the walleye has intrigued generations of fishermen. Anyone who has spent much time fishing walleyes knows that they can bite like mad one day, then disappear for the next week for no apparent reason. And when walleyes decide to quit biting, almost nothing can change their minds.

But despite their unpredictable behavior, walleyes rank among the nation's most popular gamefish. Some anglers pursue walleyes for the challenge, others because walleye fillets make prime table fare.

Originally, walleyes were found only in a triangular area extending across

Canada and south to Alabama. But as a result of widespread stocking, they are now found in almost every state and province. Few attempts have been made to introduce walleyes outside North America.

Two subspecies of walleyes have been identified in North America: the yellow walleye, *Stizostedion vitreum vitreum*, and the blue walleye or blue pike, *Stizostedion vitreum glaucum*. The

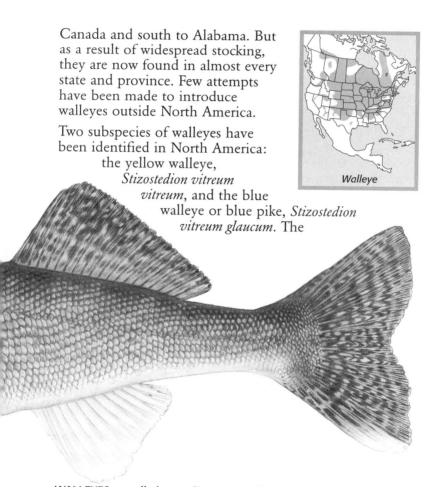

Walleye

WALLEYES usually have olive-green sides with gold flecks. The spiny dorsal fin lacks spots, but has a black rear base. The lower lobe of the tail has a white tip.

SAUGERS (above) have several rows of distinct black spots on the dorsal fin. The pectoral fins have a dark spot at the base. The overall coloration is grayish to brownish with dark blotches. There is no black area at the lower rear of the dorsal. The tail may have a thin white band at the bottom. The body is slimmer than that of a walleye.

SAUGEYES usually have a spotted dorsal fin, but the spots are not round like those of a sauger. There may be a small back area at the lower rear of the dorsal. The sides are often tinged with gold and may have faint blotches. The tail resembles that of a sauger, with no prominent white corner on the lower lobe.

yellow walleye, commonly referred to simply as walleye, is the only remaining subspecies.

Yellow walleyes (illustration, pages 28-29) usually have an olive-green back, golden sides and a white belly. Distinctive markings include a milky-white tip on the lower lobe of the tail and a black blotch at the rear base of the spiny dorsal fin.

Sauger

Coloration of walleyes varies greatly in different waters. In waters that are relatively clear, walleyes have the typical golden hue. But in bog-stained or coffee-colored waters, they are noticeably darker and often have yellowish bellies. In extremely turbid waters, walleyes usually have a grayish coloration.

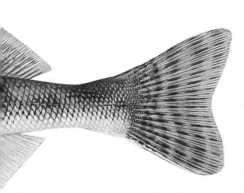

Blue walleyes had a steel-blue back, silvery sides and larger eyes. They were found only in lakes Erie and Ontario. But due to severe water pollution and excessive commercial fishing in the past, they are now thought to be extinct.

In many waters, fishermen mistake the walleye for its close relative, the sauger. But saugers have a distinctly different coloration and do not grow as large. To further complicate matters, walleyes and saugers sometimes hybridize, producing a fish called the *saugeye* with characteristics intermediate between those of the parents. Except perch and darters, walleyes have no other North American relatives. However, walleyes are closely related to the European zander, or pike-perch. The two look remarkably similar, but walleyes distribute their eggs at random while zanders are nest-builders.

The walleye's common names lead to much confusion among fishermen. In much of Canada, walleyes are called pickerel, jackfish or doré, the French name for the species. In the United States, they are often called walleyed pike. But that term is a misnomer because walleyes belong not to the pike family, but to the perch family.

Walleyes are strong but not spectacular fighters. They do not jump like bass or make sizzling runs like northern pike. Instead, they wage a dogged, head-shaking battle, stubbornly refusing to be pulled from deep water.

Throughout much of North America, anglers consider a 10-pound walleye a trophy of a lifetime. But walleyes do grow larger, sometimes twice this size. In fact, several walleyes exceeding 20 pounds have been caught in southeastern reservoirs, causing biologists to speculate that these waters contain a unique, fast-growing strain. One of the best southeastern reservoirs is Greers Ferry Lake in Arkansas. On March 14, 1982, this body of water produced a 22-pound, 11-ounce lunker, one of the largest walleyes ever recorded.

Senses

Much of the seemingly mysterious behavior of walleyes can be explained by their acute night vision, finely tuned lateral-line sense and sharp hearing. They also have a good sense of smell, but it does not appear to play a prominent role in their life.

VISION. The *tapetum lucidum*, a reflective layer of pigment in the retina, gives walleyes a built-in advantage: they can see well in dim light, but their prey cannot. This highly developed night vision explains why walleyes do most of their feeding in dim light.

QUICK TIP: Use two-tone colored jig heads to increase your chances of having the "hot" jig color for a particular day or body of water. If you are marking fish on your locator but not getting any bites, keep changing colors until the fish tell you what they prefer.

Because of their light-sensitive eyes, walleyes will not tolerate sunlight. If the water is clear and there is no shade in the shallows, they may go as deep as 40 feet to escape the penetrating rays. But in dark or choppy waters, walleyes can remain shallow all day.

Walleyes can see color, but they cannot see as many hues as fish like largemouth bass and northern pike. Any animal with good color vision has two types of color discriminating cells: red-green cells and blue-yellow cells. But a walleye lacks the blue-yellow cells, so its color vision is similar to that of the rare human beings with blue-yellow color blindness. In other words, walleyes most likely see all colors as some shade of red or green.

GLASSY EYES result from a reflective layer of pigment, called the tapetum lucidum, *in the retina. The tapetum gathers light very efficiently and accounts for the walleye's excellent night vision and aversion to bright light.*

Although walleyes can probably see reds, oranges, yellows and greens the best, water color and depth can change the way a lure appears to the fish. In addition, the best lure colors may differ from one body of water to the next because the walleyes are eating different foods. As a result, the only sure way to find the best color is to experiment.

HOW THE SENSES OF WALLEYES COMPARE TO THOSE OF OTHER GAMEFISH*

FISH SPECIES	DAYTIME VISION	NIGHT VISION
Walleye	Fair	Excellent
Sauger	Fair	Excellent
Yellow Perch	Good	Poor
Crappie	Good	Good
Bluegill	Excellent	Fair
Northern Pike	Excellent	Poor
Largemouth Bass	Good	Fair
Catfish	Fair	Fair

*Ratings determined from a survey of prominent fish physiologists and fisheries biologists.

LATERAL LINE. These ultra-sensitive nerve endings along each side of the body can detect minute vibrations in the water. The lateral-line sense enables walleyes to single out an erratically swimming baitfish from the rest of a school. The lateral line also enables them to locate an artificial lure in deep or murky water where they could not possibly see it.

HEARING. Seasoned fishermen know that walleyes in the shallows will not tolerate any commotion. Even the slightest noise will drive them into deep water. As a rule of thumb, when walleyes are in water of 10 feet or less, it pays to anchor your boat and cast to them. Avoid trolling over them, especially with an outboard motor.

Expert ice fishermen avoid drilling, or chopping holes during peak fishing periods. They know that the sound of an auger or chisel will drive the fish off their feeding reefs.

SMELL. Laboratory tests have shown that fish can detect extremely dilute odors. Yet the sense of smell does not seem to have much influence on walleye feeding behavior. If smell were important, the evidence should be most obvious in low-clarity water, where walleyes cannot see

LATERAL LINE	SMELL	HEARING
Good	Fair	Good
Excellent	Fair	Good
Fair	Fair	Fair
Fair	Fair	Fair
Fair	Good	Fair
Good	Poor	Good
Good	Fair	Good
Excellent	Excellent	Excellent

well enough to feed. But in this type of water, live bait does not work as well as artificial lures, especially lures that produce vibrations. This evidence indicates that the lateral-line sense is more significant.

The table above compares the senses of walleyes to those of other fish.

Feeding & Growth

L ike most other predatory fish, walleyes are oppor-
tunists. They eat whatever foods nature provides
them. In many mesotrophic lakes (pages 66-67),
walleyes feed primarily on yellow perch, often stalking
them at night on shoals less than 5 feet deep. In the

YELLOW PERCH make ideal prey. They have poor night vision and cannot see an approaching walleye. At night, perch rest with their fins touching bottom. Scuba divers have caught resting perch with their hands.

Missouri River reservoirs of North and South Dakota, walleyes frequently eat smelt, which they sometimes follow into water over 100 feet deep. In southern reservoirs, walleyes commonly suspend to feed on gizzard or threadfin shad, pursuing them in wide expanses of open water.

Although small fish make up the bulk of the diet in most waters, there are times when walleyes feed almost exclusively on insects, both immature and adult forms. Occasionally, walleyes eat snails, leeches, frogs, mudpuppies, crayfish and even mice.

The abundance of natural food is the major factor that determines how well walleyes bite. When food is scarce, they spend much of their time moving about in search of a meal, so the chances are greater that they will take your bait or lure. But when food is plentiful, the opposite is true.

Most species of baitfish spawn in spring. The young they produce are usually too small to interest adult walleyes until midsummer. Because yearling or adult baitfish are often scarce in spring, walleyes are hungry and fishing is

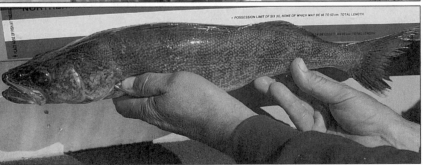

GROWTH RATES of walleyes are reflected by the size of the head compared to that of the body. A fast-growing walleye (top) has a relatively small head and a short, chunky body. A slow-growing walleye (bottom) has a relatively large head and a long, slim body.

usually good. The action slows down in summer when they begin to feed on the newly available crop of young baitfish. A commonly-heard old wives' tale is that walleyes refuse to bite in summer because they have sore mouths. But in reality, they are consuming more food than at any other time of year. Fishing picks up again in fall when predation and other natural mortality have substantially reduced the crop of young baitfish.

Fishing success in a given body of water can change dramatically from year to year, depending on whether or not there is a good baitfish hatch. Occasionally, baitfish become so abundant that walleyes are almost impossible to catch in midsummer. When baitfish are this plentiful, fishing usually remains slow through the winter months, and may stay slow through the next summer.

RECURVED TEETH make a walleye an efficient predator. A bait-fish or other prey caught by a walleye has little chance of escaping.

GROWTH RATES OF WALLEYES AT DIFFERENT LATITUDES

LAKE NAME AND LATITUDE	AGE 1	2	3
North Caribou Lake, ONT (53°N)	4.3	6.7	8.5
Lake of the Woods, MN (49°N)	5.6	8.0	10.0
Trout Lake, WI (46°N)	5.3	9.7	13.7
Spirit Lake, IA (43°N)	7.2	11.1	14.4
Pymatuning Lake, PA (42°N)	7.9	13.6	17.4
Claytor Reservoir, VA (37°N)	8.1	13.9	18.4

In some years, adverse weather prevents baitfish from spawning successfully. As a result, forage is scarce and walleyes bite well through the summer and into the winter.

How fast walleyes grow depends on the availability of food and the length of the growing season. In southern reservoirs, where shad are super-abundant and the growing season is 8 to 9 months long, walleyes can reach weights exceeding 15 pounds in only 7 years. But in the deep, cold lakes of the Canadian Shield, where baitfish are less abundant and the growing season lasts only 3 to 4 months, a walleye reaches a weight of just 2 pounds in the same amount of time.

Despite this great difference in growth rate, walleyes in northern waters can reach sizes rivaling those in the South. This phenomenon can be explained by a factor that could be called *warmwater burnout.* Fish in cold northern waters grow more slowly, but have a much longer life span than fish in warmer southern waters. Walleyes in the North have been known to live as long as 26 years, although walleyes older than 15 years are rare; in the South, a life span of 10 years would be unusual. So even though walleyes in the North do not grow as fast, their longevity results in an average size not much smaller than that in the South.

There is evidence to support the theory that a fast-growing strain of walleyes exists in rivers and reservoirs in the southeastern United States. Apparently, this strain spawns

		LENGTH IN INCHES AT VARIOUS AGES				
4	5	6	7	8	9	10
10.2	12.0	12.4	14.6	16.1	17.0	18.0
11.6	12.8	14.4	15.7	17.2	18.7	19.6
16.6	19.0	20.7	21.7	22.3	23.1	23.3
17.5	19.9	22.0	23.7	24.9	26.0	27.8
20.7	23.3	25.2	26.7	27.8	28.8	29.0
22.6	25.5	27.4	30.0	32.2	—	—

exclusively in rivers. When dams were built to create the reservoirs, long stretches of river habitat were lost. In most cases, the walleyes eventually disappeared from the reservoirs.

Many of these reservoirs were then stocked with northern-strain walleyes. This strain can spawn in rivers or lakes, but evidently does not grow as fast as the southern strain. In Center Hill Reservoir, Tennessee, southern-strain walleyes sampled in 1964 averaged 30.6 inches (about 10½ pounds) at age 7. They eventually disappeared from the reservoir, so it was stocked with northern-strain walleyes. When the northern fish were sampled in 1976, they averaged only 23.3 inches (about 4½ pounds) at age 7.

Female walleyes grow much faster, live longer and attain much larger sizes than males. In most waters, male walleyes exceeding 4 pounds are unusual.

Habitat Preferences

Compared to most other freshwater fish, walleyes can tolerate an exceptionally wide range of environmental conditions. This explains why they are found from northern Canada to the southern United States. Most of the habitat preferences of the walleye are described below. Another important factor, light level, is discussed on pages 50-51.

TEMPERATURE. The walleye is a coolwater species, meaning that it prefers intermediate temperatures when compared to warmwater fish like bass and coldwater fish

(1) Walleyes concentrate around the mouth of an inlet stream because of the reduced clarity. (2) Walleyes prefer a firm bottom, usually sand, gravel, rock or a combination of these materials. (3) No walleyes on soft, mucky bottom, even though it is in the right temperature zone. (4) No walleyes in deep hole

like trout. In summer, walleyes are commonly found at temperatures from 65° to 75°F, but they will leave this zone to find food or to avoid intense light. At other times of year, they will usually seek the water closest to their preferred summer range. Walleyes are seldom found at temperatures above 80°F.

WATER CLARITY. Walleyes prefer water of relatively low clarity. They are most abundant where suspended silt or algae, or bog stain, limits visibility to about 3 to 6 feet. Tannic acid and other dissolved organic materials are responsible for the bog-stained, or coffee-colored, appearance of many lakes in the North.

Differences in clarity within the same body of water may affect walleye location. In a clear lake, researchers found that walleyes were 10 times more abundant in the turbid zone near a river mouth than in other parts of the lake. But in low-clarity lakes, walleyes generally avoid highly turbid areas.

BOTTOM TYPE. Given a choice, walleyes generally select clean, hard bottoms rather than bottoms of silt, muck or other soft materials. Walleyes favor bottoms

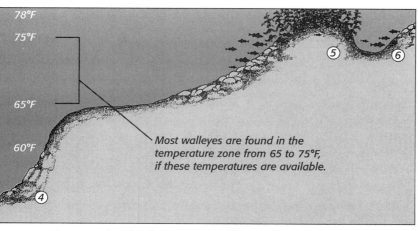

Most walleyes are found in the temperature zone from 65 to 75°F, if these temperatures are available.

because the depths are too cold and often lack sufficient dissolved oxygen. (5) Walleyes are drawn into trough between sunken island and shore by wind-induced currents. (6) Shallow, rocky shoreline exposed to the wind makes excellent spawning habitat.

with a combination of sand, gravel and rock. This type of bottom produces a great deal of insect and other invertebrate life, which in turn attracts baitfish.

In fertile lakes, the bottom is often covered with a thick layer of soft sediment. Experienced anglers know that if they can find an exposed rock pile or gravel bar, it will usually hold walleyes.

A study conducted on the Mississippi River revealed that walleye populations declined as shoreline protected by riprap, or large rock, was covered with sand from Corps of Engineers dredging. Populations remained stable where the riprap banks were still exposed.

SPAWNING HABITAT. Shallow, rocky shorelines and reefs make ideal spawning habitat. The eggs fall into crevices between the rocks where they are safe from crayfish and other egg-eating predators. Spawning is most successful in large lakes because the spawning habitat is exposed to the wind. Some wave action is necessary to prevent the eggs from silting over and to keep them aerated. So it is not surprising that lakes of this type have the highest walleye populations. Walleyes can also spawn in rivers and streams, if there is enough rocky bottom.

Many fertile lakes and reservoirs lack suitable spawning areas. A few walleyes may spawn along shorelines where homeowners have placed rocks to protect the bank, or on flooded gravel roadbeds. Unless these waters are stocked, they seldom contain many walleyes.

OXYGEN. Walleyes avoid water with a dissolved oxygen content below 4 ppm (parts per million). But contrary to popular belief, they do not seek out areas with higher oxygen levels. It is true that windswept portions of a lake draw the most walleyes. However, the fish are attracted by lower light levels and a concentration of food, not by higher oxygen.

Walleyes can tolerate oxygen levels as low as 1 ppm for short periods. It is not unusual for walleyes to move into deep water with a low oxygen level, especially when there is an easy source of food in the depths or water in the shallows becomes too warm.

CURRENT. Walleyes are native to most major river systems in the North, so they are accustomed to living in current.

Given a choice, lake-dwelling walleyes will seek areas of light current rather than stay in slack water. The highest walleye concentrations are often found around inlet streams, in narrows separating two basins of a lake or in areas with wind-induced currents.

pH. This is a term used to denote the acidity or alkalinity of the water. pH is measured on a scale from 1 to 14, with 1 the most acidic and 14 the most alkaline. A pH of 7 is neutral. Fishing waters usually have pH levels ranging from 6 to 9. If the pH drops below 5.5, walleye eggs do not develop properly, so the fish eventually disappear.

Canadian researchers have found that adult walleyes avoid pH levels below 6 or above 9. But within that range, pH has no effect on walleye behavior. Because the walleye's pH comfort range corresponds to the range found in most waters, there is no need to concern yourself with pH.

Spawning Behavior

In early spring, as the days grow longer and the water temperature rises, walleyes know that the time has come to abandon their winter haunts and begin their annual spawning migration.

Walleyes can spawn successfully in natural lakes, reservoirs and rivers. In many cases, some walleyes spawn in the main body of a lake or reservoir while others spawn in tributary streams.

Spawning areas are usually 1 to 6 feet deep, with a bottom of gravel to baseball-sized rock. Because the eggs require constant aeration, walleyes in lakes and reservoirs deposit their eggs on shoal areas exposed to the wind. River walleyes usually spawn in areas with moderate current. Seldom will walleyes spawn in a sheltered bay or backwater.

Male walleyes are the first to move into the vicinity of the spawning area. Large numbers of males gather even though the water temperature may be only a few degrees above freezing, and spawning time is a month or more away. Females begin moving in several weeks later, when the water temperature reaches the upper 30s to low 40s.

Walleyes remain relatively deep until spawning time approaches. A week or two before spawning, they move shallower and begin to feed more heavily. On warm evenings, they mill about in the spawning area, then drop back to slightly deeper water when the sun comes up. These nighttime movements become more frequent as spawning time nears.

The exact water temperature at which walleyes spawn depends on latitude. Walleyes in the North may spawn at temperatures as much as 15 degrees lower than in the

MALE walleyes bump the sides of the female during the spawning act, emitting milt while she drops her eggs. Sometimes several males bump a single female. A female deposits 50,000 to 300,000 eggs, usually in a single night. Fertilized eggs fall between the rocks where they are safe from egg-eating predators. Parents abandon the eggs after spawning. On a rocky bottom, up to 25 percent of the eggs will hatch; on soft muck, less than 1 percent.

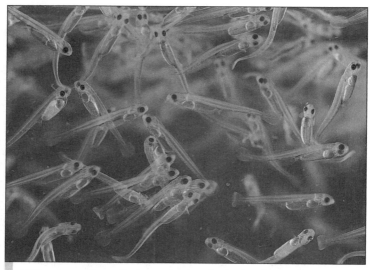

FRY emerge from the eggs in 1 to 2 weeks, depending on water temperature. They live off the egg sac for the first few days of life. On the average, only 1 fry in 1,000 survives to fingerling size.

South. In the extreme northern part of their range, walleyes generally spawn at temperatures from 40° to 44°F; in the South, from 50° to 55°F.

Spawning times can differ by as much as two weeks in waters in the same area. A shallow lake, for instance, warms much faster than a deep one, so walleyes spawn much sooner.

Because offshore waters warm more slowly, spawning on reefs may take place as much as 2 weeks later than spawning on shorelines and in tributaries.

The spawning period generally lasts from 1 to 2 weeks. But if the water warms rapidly, walleyes spawn at temperatures higher than normal and all spawning is completed in a few days. If the water warms slowly, they start to spawn at temperatures lower than normal and spawning activity may continue for 3 weeks or more. A severe cold snap during the spawning period may interrupt spawning for several days. After repeated cold snaps, walleyes may reabsorb their eggs and not spawn at all.

FINGERLING size, 4 to 8 inches, is reached by the end of the summer. About 5 to 10 percent of the fingerlings survive to catchable size, although survival rates vary greatly in different types of waters.

Although an individual female usually drops all of her eggs on the same night, not all females ripen at once. This explains why some walleyes are just beginning to spawn when others have been finished for a week or more.

After spawning is completed, males stay near the spawning area up to a month and continue to feed. Females begin to move toward their early-summer locations soon after spawning. When recuperating, they refuse food for about 2 weeks. But after recuperation, they begin a period of heavy feeding that lasts for several weeks. Anglers who know where to find them during this post-spawn feeding spree enjoy some of the best fishing of the year, particularly for trophy-class walleyes.

How Light Level Affects Walleyes

ight level is the single most important influence on walleye behavior. It determines when and where walleyes feed, and where they spend their time when not feeding. Most anglers know that walleyes have light-sensitive eyes and shy away from bright sunlight, but they do not fully understand how light level affects their fishing.

The angle at which sunlight strikes the water determines how much of the light will penetrate. When the surface is calm and the sun just above the horizon, most of the rays are reflected. If the sun is directly overhead, most of the rays penetrate.

Sun angle can have different effects in different waters, depending on clarity. In low-clarity water, suspended particles or dissolved organic matter filter out sunlight, keeping light levels in shallow feeding areas relatively low.

The time of day at which walleyes feed may be much different in spring and fall than in summer. On the first day of spring and fall, the angle at which the sun strikes the water at 9 A.M. at the latitude of Lake Erie is about 30 degrees. On the first day of summer, the angle is about 50 degrees. In spring and fall, as a result, morning feeding periods last later into the day and afternoon feeding periods start earlier.

Weather conditions also affect the amount of light that penetrates the water. Although walleyes in clear water generally feed at dusk or dawn, an overcast sky or choppy surface can reduce the light level enough to allow some midday feeding. In some waters, heavy cover like boulders or tall weeds provides enough shade for occasional feeding during the middle of the day.

Canadian researchers have proven that the rate at which light intensity changes is the most important factor in triggering walleyes to feed. In a moderately clear lake, walleyes bit best as the sun rose above the horizon in the morning and as it disappeared below the horizon in the evening. Light intensity changed at a lower rate immediately before and after these periods, and walleyes bit at a significantly slower pace. This research also explains why walleyes bite so well when a storm is approaching.

HOW THE EFFECTS OF LIGHT DIFFER IN CLEAR AND MURKY WATER
(examples are for clear skies and calm water surface)

•*Clear water.* At dawn and dusk, the light level is ideal, so walleyes feed heavily in the shallows. In midmorning and midafternoon, light intensity is high enough to drive them deeper and slow their feeding. At midday, the intense light forces them into deep water and causes them to stop feeding.

•*Murky water.* At dawn and dusk, walleyes are in the shallows, but the light level is too low for feeding. In midmorning and midafternoon, the light level is ideal. Walleyes remain in the shallows and feed heavily. At midday, light intensity is high enough to drive them slightly deeper and to slow feeding.

HOW WALLEYES REACT TO DIFFERENT LIGHT CONDITIONS
(results of a test done on walleyes in a large fish tank)

•*Bright light.* When exposed to a powerful spotlight held directly overhead, walleyes lie flat on the bottom. They remain virtually motionless, stabilizing themselves with their pectoral fins.

•*Dim light.* When the light is turned off, the walleyes slowly become active. After about 20 minutes, they move about continuously in the tank. They spend much of their time a foot or more above the bottom.

•*Shade.* With the light directly overhead, a board is placed over part of the tank. The walleyes move to the shaded area. They move about somewhat more than they did in bright light.

•*Angled light.* The light is moved to the side of the tank so that it strikes the water at a 30-degree angle. Much of the light is reflected, so the light intensity is relatively low and the walleyes are fairly active.

How Weather Affects Walleye Behavior

Weather can be a walleye fisherman's greatest ally or his greatest foe. Exactly how weather affects walleyes, however, is a topic on which few anglers concur. Although there has been little scientific research on the influence of weather on walleye behavior, most expert anglers believe the following:

•*The best walleye fishing* results from conditions that cause rapidly decreasing light levels. For instance, a sudden increase in wind velocity creates a walleye chop which scatters the light waves and often triggers a feeding spree. Similarly, dark clouds from an approaching thunderstorm usually start a period of frenzied feeding.

•*Wind direction* can have a dramatic effect on where walleyes in a given body of water will be most likely to bite. In a

IDEAL WALLEYE WEATHER for waters that are relatively clear usually consists of a moderate chop and overcast skies. On a typical overcast day, only one-fourth as much light reaches the surface as would on a sunny day. Choppy water scatters the rays so that much less light penetrates. Because of the low light level, walleyes may feed throughout the day. In highly turbid water, ideal walleye weather is calm and sunny.

clear lake, for example, walleyes may feed along windward shores while fishing on the lee side of the lake is poor. Silt churned up by the wave action reduces the light level enough to allow shallow-water feeding.

Wind can also cause currents in narrows or around reefs and points, concentrating food and attracting walleyes. Wind-induced currents can wash food off a reef and draw walleyes to the downwind side.

Cloudy or rainy weather usually spells good walleye fishing. But where the water is extremely turbid, heavy cloud

cover or the disturbance caused by raindrops striking the surface may keep the light level too low for walleyes to feed.

•Walleye fishing is generally good during periods of stable weather because the fish maintain fairly predictable feeding patterns.

•The poorest fishing follows the passage of a severe cold front or an intense thunderstorm, especially if there are frequent lightning strikes.

After a severe cold front, the sky often becomes exceptionally clear. Because there is no haze to filter out the sun's rays, 10 to 20 percent more light penetrates than normally would. This condition causes walleyes to stop feeding and move deeper or seek cover beneath the weeds.

•For some unknown reason, cold fronts and thunderstorms seem to have less effect on walleyes in rivers than in lakes.

•Calm, sunny weather in a clear body of water makes walleyes stop biting earlier than usual in the morning and start later than usual in the afternoon. But in low-clarity water, it makes them begin feeding earlier in the morning and continue later into the afternoon.

> QUICK TIP: Rather than struggle to catch one or two walleyes on a bright sunny day on a clear lake, wait until sunset to begin fishing. You may have to deal with more bug bites by fishing after dark, but your reward will be a lot more walleyes.

In clear waters that do not stratify (page 65), walleyes may feed in midday in calm, sunny weather. Because there is no thermocline, they can simply move as deep as necessary to avoid sunlight.

•There is no evidence that barometric pressure play a major role in walleye fishing. Some walleye experts believe that the fish bite best when the barometer is rapidly falling. But the increase in feeding activity is more likely the result of the decreasing light intensity associated with an approaching storm.

POOR CONDITIONS FOR WALLEYE FISHING

•*Lightning* accompanied by loud thunderclaps makes walleyes bury in the weeds or move deeper. If lightning

HOW WIND DIRECTION AFFECTS WALLEYE FISHING

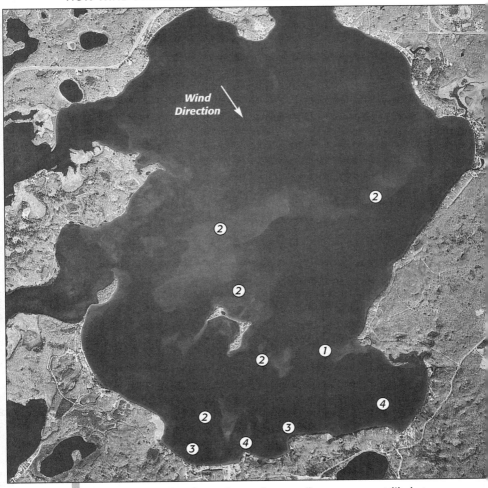

Wind Direction

WIND DIRECTION determines where walleyes are most likely to be feeding. With a northwest wind, for example, walleyes in the lake shown above would feed most heavily in the following areas: (1) a gradually sloping point and (2) shallow reefs, all exposed to the wind. Walleyes in these areas are triggered to feed by reduced clarity from wave action, wind-induced currents and food washed loose from the bottom. Walleyes also feed in (3) inside turns on the breakline that gather windblown plankton which in turn attract baitfish, and (4) bays on the south end that trap warm surface water blown in by the wind, resulting in temperatures a few degrees higher than on the other end of the lake. The warm water draws baitfish, especially in spring.

HOW TO SELECT A LAKE ON THE BASIS OF WIND DIRECTION

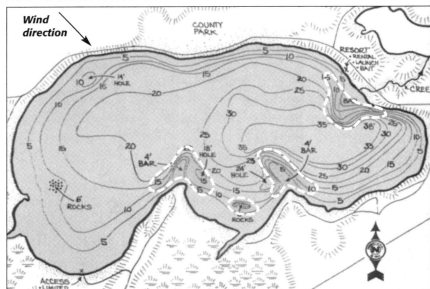

CHECK the weather forecast before deciding where you are going to fish. With a northwest wind, for example, the lake above would be a better choice than the one on the opposite page, all other factors being equal. The best walleye structure (dotted regions) is on the southeast side, so a northwest wind

and thunder continue for several hours, the fish may not feed regularly for the next 2 or 3 days.

•*Cool, blustery weather* following a cold front makes walleyes very sluggish. They generally move deeper and refuse food. Like a thunderstorm, a cold front can slow fishing for 2 or 3 days.

GOOD CONDITIONS FOR WALLEYE FISHING

•*Dark clouds* from an approaching storm cause the light level to decrease rapidly, making walleyes bite faster than at any other time. But be sure to get off the water before the storm arrives.

•*Roily water* along a windswept shore is a good spot for walleyes to feed in a clear lake. The waves stir up silt,

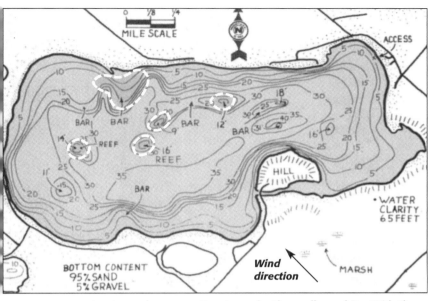

creates enough wave action to make the walleyes bite. With the same wind, the lake on this page would be a poor choice because the best structure is on the northwest side where it is sheltered from the wind. But this lake would be a better choice with a southeast wind.

decreasing the light level. They also dislodge bottom organisms which attract baitfish.

How Moon Phase Affects Walleye Fishing

There has been no scientific research on the effects of moon phase on walleye fishing. To determine if moon phase is an important factor for walleye anglers to consider, the researchers for this book conducted a poll of experienced walleye fishermen throughout the country.

The results of that poll are difficult to summarize because there were nearly as many differing opinions as there were

MOON PHASE does not seem to affect the total number of big walleyes caught at different times of the month, but it may affect the time of day when walleye fishing is best. Although the most big walleyes were caught around the full moon and the least around the first quarter moon, the numbers are not different enough to draw any conclusions on the best fishing time. Figures for each quarter phase include the number of walleyes caught in 7 days of the 28-day lunar cycle. The full moon period, for instance, includes 3 days on either side of the full moon.

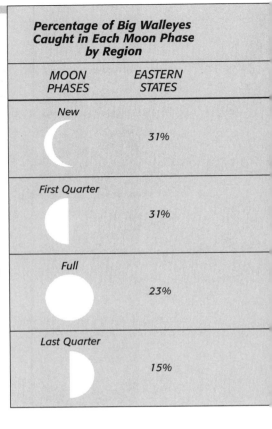

Percentage of Big Walleyes Caught in Each Moon Phase by Region	
MOON PHASES	EASTERN STATES
New	31%
First Quarter	31%
Full	23%
Last Quarter	15%

interviews. The effects of the moon seemed to be different in clear lakes than in waters of low clarity.

Many of the anglers who fished on clear lakes believed that daytime fishing was best around the full moon, but that night fishing was poorest. They also believed that daytime fishing was poorest around the new moon, but that night fishing was best.

The majority of anglers who fished in low-clarity waters thought the opposite. That is, they believed that daytime fishing was best and night fishing poorest around the new moon. And most of them thought that daytime fishing was poorest and night fishing best around the full moon. These opinions suggest that the effects of the moon are more related to light level than to gravitational pull.

SOUTH-CENTRAL STATES	NORTH-CENTRAL STATES	WESTERN STATES	NATIONWIDE
18%	31%	25%	26%
25%	17%	18%	21%
21%	28%	39%	28%
36%	24%	18%	25%

Almost all fishermen interviewed agreed on one point: the effects of local weather conditions may override any influences of the moon.

Theoretically, the effects of moon phase should be most noticeable on trophy-sized walleyes because they are much more cautious than small ones and more affected by subtle environmental changes. Researchers compiled records from throughout the United States of the biggest walleyes caught by angling, then correlated these catches to moon phase. The results are shown on the chart above.

Typical Walleye Waters

Walleyes exist in waters ranging in size from tiny natural lakes of 50 acres or less to the western basin of Lake Erie, sprawling over 1,265 square miles. They are found in fertile lakes of pea-soup clarity to

MESOTROPHIC LAKES (pages 66-67) generally harbor the largest walleye populations. The moderately fertile water produces good food crops, so walleyes grow fairly fast. Most of

ultra-clear lakes of the Canadian Shield. And they are equally comfortable in still or flowing water.

Natural lakes provide far more walleye habitat than any other type of water. In terms of total acreage, North American walleye waters break down as follows: 94 percent natural lakes, 5 percent man-made reservoirs and 1 percent rivers and streams.

As a result of widespread stocking outside their native range, walleyes are now found in 32 percent of all the freshwater acreage in North America.

Populations are usually highest in large, shallow bodies of water with moderate to low clarity. A large expanse of

these lakes have enough gravel or rubble bottom for successful spawning. Meso lakes seldom winter-kill, but may lack oxygen in the depths.

OLIGOTROPHIC LAKES (pages 68-70) have fair to good walleye populations. Their waters are usually cold and infertile, but their rocky basins make good spawning habitat. Walleyes in these lakes grow more slowly, but live longer than in warmer water. Most oligotrophic lakes are in remote areas, so anglers take fewer walleyes.

water is likely to have the windswept shorelines and reefs that make ideal spawning habitat. And shallow water provides more food than deep water. If the shoreline drops sharply into the depths and has few shallow feeding shelves, chances are walleyes will not be abundant. Waters of relatively low clarity limit sunlight penetration and shield the walleye's light-sensitive eyes.

Along with the basic types of natural lakes shown in photographs in this section, the other important types of walleye waters are as follows:

MID-DEPTH RESERVOIRS (pages 72-74) usually have tremendous baitfish crops. Walleyes exceeding the world record have recently been netted and released in waters of this type. Mid-depth reservoirs have numerous coves, or creek arms, extending from the main body.

SHALLOW RESERVOIRS (pages 74-76), called *flowages* in the North, often have basins with little structure. These man-made lakes have fertile water and produce large num-

EUTROPHIC LAKES (pages 71-72) are highly fertile and have abundant food supplies. Walleyes grow rapidly, but because the silted basins offer limited spawning habitat, natural populations are seldom high. In most cases, these lakes must be stocked. If the lake is less than 25 feet deep, heavy snow cover may cause frequent winterkills.

bers of walleyes, although big ones are not as common as in mid-depth reservoirs.

BIG RIVERS (pages 76-78), especially those with abundant backwater areas, often hold good numbers of large walleyes. The backwaters produce large quantities of food, provide nursery areas for young walleyes and give adult walleyes a place to escape the current.

MEDIUM-SIZED RIVERS (pages 78-79) can support walleyes if there are rocky areas for spawning and deep pools for wintering. Although food is plentiful, walleyes run smaller than in most other waters because much of their energy is wasted in fighting the current.

Where to Find Walleyes through the Seasons

To catch walleyes consistently, you must know where to find them at different times of the year. In this section, we will trace their movements from early spring through late fall.

SPRING. In early spring, walleyes often travel great distances to reach their spawning areas. In large lakes and reservoirs and in big river systems, migrations of over 50 miles are not uncommon.

Walleyes have a strong homing instinct. An individual fish will usually return to spawn in the same area each year. Once you discover a heavily used spawning area, chances are you will find walleyes there in subsequent years. The locations where walleyes spawn are described on pages 46-49.

Once walleyes recover from spawning, they move gradually toward their summer haunts, scattering as the water temperature warms. During this period, food becomes the major driving force in their lives. They spend most of their time in shallow water, where baitfish and other foods are most plentiful. Because the previous year's baitfish crop has been drastically reduced by predation and the current year's crop is not yet available, walleyes may have to roam the shallows all day to find enough food. They can comfortably remain in the shallows because surface temperatures are still cool, and the angle of the sun is low enough to make light levels tolerable.

SUMMER. By midsummer, baitfish hatched in spring have grown large enough to interest walleyes. Because food is much easier to find, it has less influence on walleye location. The fish can spend more of their time in deeper water where temperatures are cooler and light levels more to their liking.

Most walleye waters stratify into temperature layers in summer. The *thermocline*, the layer where the water temperature changes rapidly, separates the warm upper layer, or *epilimnion*, from the cold lower layer, or *hypolimnion*.

In the far North, the epilimnion remains cool enough for walleyes. But further south, the upper portion of the thermocline is most likely to have the moderate temperatures that walleyes prefer.

Some walleye waters do not stratify into temperature layers, so the fish are less likely to stay at a specific depth. Rivers, reservoirs with a large quantity of inflowing water, and shallow, windswept lakes seldom form temperature layers.

Oxygen supply affects summertime walleye location in some shallow to medium-depth lakes and reservoirs. If these waters stratify, the hypolimnion loses oxygen in summer. Because the cold water in the depths is heavier than the warm water in the shallows, the wind does not circulate the deep water and replenish its oxygen supply. Plankton, fish and other organisms use up what oxygen there is, making water below the thermocline off limits to walleyes, except for occasional feeding forays.

FALL. Walleyes spend more time in the shallows when the surface water starts to cool. As the season progresses, more and more young-of-the-year baitfish fall victim to predation. Because food is again harder to find, walleyes must spend more time searching the shallows. They can stay in shallow water because the sun is again lower in the sky and the light level is less intense.

When the surface temperature cools enough to match the temperature in the depths, wind circulates the water from top to bottom. This mixing process is called the *fall turnover*. With temperature and oxygen levels equal throughout, walleyes can be found almost anywhere.

By late fall, the surface temperature is colder than that in the depths, so walleyes move deeper to find water closer to their preferred temperature range. They often hold near sharp drop-offs, where they can quickly move into shallower water to feed.

In waters that do not freeze in winter, walleyes generally remain where they were in late fall. They become less active as the winter wears on, but a period of warm, sunny weather may draw them into shallower water in search of food. In late winter, they become more active again.

Mesotrophic Lakes

The term *mesotrophic* means middle fertility. And it is true that these natural lakes have fertility levels between those of *oligotrophic* (scant fertility) and *eutrophic* (good fertility) lakes. In most cases, mesotrophic lakes are also intermediate in depth, temperature and clarity.

In mesotrophic lakes, walleye spawning habitat is usually abundant. Many such lakes are fed by streams that have clean gravel or rock bottoms and enough deep pockets to hold walleyes on their spring migration. In some cases, walleyes spawn in outlet streams as well as inlets. They can also spawn in the lake itself, along shallow, windswept shorelines and reefs. Many mesotrophic lakes have populations of both lake- and stream-spawning walleyes.

Stream spawners gather near the mouths of inlets when the main body of the lake is still covered with ice. After the ice goes out, lake spawners collect just off the breaklines along the spawning shoals.

Because water in the streams warms faster than water in the lake, stream spawning takes place a week or two earlier than lake spawning.

Soon after spawning is completed, stream spawners move back to the lake. Lake spawners retreat to deeper water near spawning shoals. Males remain near stream mouths or spawning shoals for up to a month. Females move away from the shoals soon after spawning. They concentrate around points, irregularities on the breakline, or the base of offshore spawning reefs. Some can be found in mud-bottomed bays with pockets at least 15 feet deep.

As summer approaches, most walleyes move to gradually sloping offshore structure. If none is available, they remain near shoreline points and irregular portions of the break-line. After moving to their summer locations, they gorge themselves on baitfish or immature insects. This period of extremely heavy feeding lasts about 2 weeks. In many lakes, anglers catch more big walleyes during this period than during the rest of the year combined.

The edge of the weedline is a prime summertime location in many mesotrophic lakes. Often, the weedline forms at approximately the same depth as the upper portion of the thermocline, providing walleyes comfortable temperatures and shade. In dim light periods, they feed in shallower water adjacent to their daytime hideouts. As the summer progresses, they spend more time feeding at night and less during the day.

In early fall, walleyes begin to comb the shallows in search of baitfish, scattering over large flats rather than holding tightly to structure. They continue this pattern until the fall turnover.

Mesotrophic lakes generally turn over later than nearby eutrophic lakes, but earlier than oligotrophic lakes. Fishing is difficult during the turnover because the fish are scattered and they can be at practically any depth.

After the turnover, walleyes form tight schools on structure that has a large, shallow feeding shelf on top and a sharp break leading to deep water. The deep water offers the most comfortable temperatures in late fall. But despite the cold surface temperature, walleyes spend a good deal of time in the shallows, feeding heavily in preparation for winter.

PRIME LOCATIONS TO FIND WALLEYES IN MESOTROPHIC LAKES:

•*Inlet streams,* particularly those with clear rock or gravel bottoms, are ideal for walleye spawning.

•*Open water* at the mouth of an inlet stream draws large concentrations of walleyes prior to spawning.

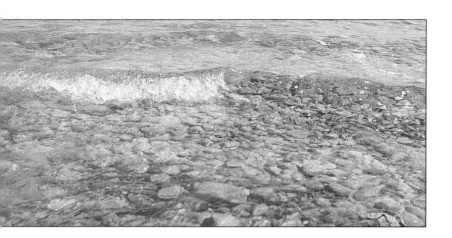

•*Gravel-rubble shorelines (above),* especially those exposed to the wind, make excellent spawning habitat.

•*Gradually tapering points* in the vicinity of the spawning grounds attract post-spawn walleye.

•*Shallow reefs,* especially large ones with a slow taper, draw walleyes in the early part of the summer.

•*Deep reefs,* particularly those connected to other structure by a saddle, are good midsummer spots.

•*Irregular breaklines* hold more walleyes in summer than a breakline with few points or indentations.

•*Long, weedy points* extending into the main part of the lake draw good numbers of walleyes in summer.

•*Sharp-dropping points* in the main lake produce walleyes from mid-fall to late fall.

•*Bulrush beds* on shallow points and reefs draw walleyes in spring and late fall. Fish hold along the edges.

Oligotrophic Lakes

Many of these low-fertility natural lakes have steep-sloping shorelines that are unsuitable for spawning, so most walleyes spawn in inlet streams. They may spawn in the lake itself, if there are shallow, rocky shorelines or reefs.

Walleyes begin to gather near their spawning grounds two to three weeks before spawning begins.

Stream spawners congregate on flats where a stream flows into the lake. As the water warms, they gradually begin to move upstream. The migration continues until the water becomes too shallow or until they reach a dam or natural barrier.

If the stream is deep enough or the water dark enough, walleyes will remain in the stream during the day, holding in deep pools. But if the pools are shallow enough that you can see bottom, chances are the walleyes will move back to the lake during daylight hours. They spawn at night, usually in shallow, rocky areas with moderate current. In some years, spawning may take place before the main lake is free of ice. After spawning, the females quickly return to the lake; some males remain near the spawning area for up to a month.

Lake spawning begins a week or two later than stream spawning. Pre-spawn walleyes hold on breaks leading from deep water to spawning areas. The fish deposit their eggs in areas exposed to prevailing winds. Females leave the spawning area almost immediately; males remain for about two weeks.

After leaving their spawning areas, both lake and stream spawners usually move to bays from 15 to 30 feet deep. There they find warmer water and a good supply of food like insect larvae and baitfish. Walleyes generally remain in the bays for four to six weeks before moving to the main lake. If the bay is deep enough, some may remain all summer.

After walleyes begin filtering out of the shallow bays, look for them on points, flats and other shoreline structure near the bay entrances. Later in the summer, many of the fish move away from shoreline structure and onto gradually sloping reefs in deep water. The best reefs usually top off at a depth of 20 feet or less. Sandy, weed-covered reefs in an otherwise rocky basin often draw more walleyes than rocky reefs.

During the summer, walleyes feed only for short periods each day. Because the water is so clear, sunlight penetration in the shallows keeps them off the feeding reefs during the day, except in windy or overcast weather.

In lakes with good populations of ciscoes, big walleyes often suspend in the lower portion of the thermocline in summer. Although the water is cooler than walleyes prefer, they will take advantage of this easy source of food.

When the water begins to cool in early fall, walleyes start to feed in shallow water. But as cooling continues, they move out of the shallows and form tight schools on structure that breaks more sharply. These schools can be very difficult to find, but if you can locate one, the fish will usually bite.

Oligotrophic lakes turn over later than nearby mesotrophic lakes. Because the deep water is so cold, it takes a long time for the surface to reach the same temperature. Most anglers avoid these lakes during the turnover period. When walleyes are scattered in cold water, they become nearly impossible to catch. You may be able to take some fish after turnover by fishing reefs that top off at 30 to 45 feet.

Waterfalls (above) in spawning streams on oligotrophic lakes block upstream migration. Large numbers of walleyes spawn below the falls.

Eutrophic Lakes

Walleyes in these high-fertility natural lakes usually spawn on gravelly shorelines in the lake proper or in the lower reaches of inlet streams. These streams are often shallow and silted in, so walleyes do not stay in them throughout the spawning period. Instead, they swim in at night and move back to the lake before morning.

Before spawning, walleyes cruise breaklines near the area where they will spawn. They tend to move more in these lakes than they would in lakes that have more structure.

After spawning, walleyes scatter throughout the lake. Look for them around points, breakline irregularities and areas where the drop-off is most distinct, or near clumps of weeds on flats adjacent to the breakline. The largest concentrations will still be found on breaklines near the spawning site.

GRAVEL POINTS and shallow, gravelly shorelines of eutrophic lakes make good spawning habitat if they are exposed to the wind.

As summer approaches, some walleyes move away from shoreline structure to mid-lake reefs and sunken islands. But many eutrophic lakes do not have this type of structure, so walleyes stay in their postspawn locations throughout the summer.

Walleyes in eutrophic lakes are strongly attracted to submerged weeds in summer, especially if the weeds are growing on a firm bottom. These weeds hold baitfish and insects in addition to providing shade. Often, walleyes move into the densest part of a weedbed, where they are nearly impossible to catch.

In most eutrophic lakes, walleyes stay shallow through the summer, often no deeper than 15 feet. Many eutrophic lakes do not stratify, but in those that do, the hypolimnion lacks sufficient oxygen. As a result, walleyes cannot venture below the thermocline for extended periods. Suspended plankton cut light penetration enough that walleyes can stay shallow without the sunlight affecting their eyes.

Soon after surface temperatures begin to cool in fall, the lake turns over. The fall turnover takes place much earlier in shallow lakes than in deep lakes because the surface temperature must drop only a few degrees to equal the bottom temperature. Because the turnover causes only a slight temperature change, its effects are less drastic than in a deeper lake. In most cases, the fish remain in the same areas where they were in summer.

In late fall, look for walleyes along sharp drop-offs adjacent to shallow feeding shelves. They usually begin feeding in mid-morning, slow down in early afternoon, then feed heavily in late afternoon. They spend most of the day in deep water because the temperature is warmer than in the shallows. Also, the cold temperature has caused plankton to die off, allowing more sunlight to penetrate.

Mid-Depth Reservoirs

These mid-depth, man-made lakes vary greatly in size and shape depending on the surrounding terrain. Many are located in hilly or mountainous country, and have an

Rocky points in the main body of the reservoir are prime summertime walleye locations, especially if the points have shallow feeding shelves.

irregular basin with many creek arms, or coves. Mid-depth reservoirs are generally intermediate in fertility, temperature and clarity, compared to shallow reservoirs and deep canyon reservoirs.

Most of the walleyes spawn in streams flowing into the coves or in the main river entering the reservoir. Walleyes may run upstream for miles, until a rapids or dam blocks their progress. If there are no suitable streams, they spawn along riprap shorelines, dam facings or bridge and causeway embankments.

Weeks before spawning time, walleyes move into cove mouths. When early spring rains cause the streamflow to increase, the fish begin moving up the cove, then into the flowing portion of the stream.

Walleyes generally spawn at night in shallow riffles or runs, particularly those that drop off into pools at least 10 feet deep. During the day, they remain in the pools.

After spawning, males stay in the stream for about two weeks, then move back to the cove. Females begin moving back almost immediately. In the cove, walleyes gather on shallow points and timbered flats along the old creek channel. Because the fish are holding in a small area and feeding heavily, the postspawn period offers some of the year's fastest action.

Walleyes stay in the coves for about two or three weeks before moving out to the main body of the reservoir. But if there is enough deep water in the cove, some may remain there through winter.

Once walleyes leave the coves, they can be difficult to find. Look for them around rocky points in the main lake or on reefs that top off at 15 to 25 feet. Many reservoirs stratify in summer. Although the surface water may exceed 85°F, walleyes can find comfortable temperatures in the thermocline.

The water level is often lowered in fall to make room for spring runoff. Following this drawdown, spots that held walleyes in summer may be dry. The fish are more closely linked to the old river channel, especially to areas of the channel with sharp-tapering points or other fast-sloping structure.

Many walleyes gather around the mouths of spawning coves in late fall. They stay in these areas through the winter, feeding on points at the cove mouth during periods of warm weather.

Shallow Reservoirs

These highly fertile man-made lakes are usually found in areas of flat terrain. Spawning habitat may be scarce because the tributary streams and lake bottom are silted in from soil erosion. Some flowages in the North have tributaries with enough deep water and clean bottom for successful spawning.

If the streams and shoreline are too silty, walleyes will spawn on whatever rock or gravel bottom they can find. Often, they have no choice but to spawn on old roadbeds or the riprap facing of the dam.

Before spawning, walleyes gather in deep water adjacent to their spawning areas. If the spawning area is close to the old river channel, they usually hold in deep portions of the channel until warming water draws them into the shallows.

The upper ends of most shallow reservoirs have extensive mud flats, formed by an accumulation of silt from inflowing streams. Because of the shallow water and dark bottom, the mud flats warm quickly in spring. When walleyes recover from spawning, they can easily find food on the flats because the warm water attracts baitfish. Walleyes that spawned on the dam facing will often swim the entire length of the reservoir to reach these flats.

Rocky or brush-covered points protruding into the old river channel will also draw walleyes after spawning. Some walleyes remain near these points through the summer.

In some shallow reservoirs, the deep water lacks oxygen in summer, so walleyes are confined to depths less than 15 feet. Even if the deep water has sufficient oxygen, the low clarity keeps walleyes shallow most of the time. You can find them along edges of the old river channel or on submerged hilltops near the channel, especially in areas with a firm sand or gravel bottom. If the reservoir has timber along the channel margins, walleyes seek shade among the trees and stumps.

Mud flats at the upper end of a shallow reservoir attract walleyes after spawning because they offer warmer temperatures than deeper areas.

The same types of structure continue to hold walleyes into fall, but as the temperature cools, they begin seeking out areas with sharper breaks. By late fall, most have moved out of the timber. If the reservoir is drawn down in fall, walleyes concentrate in deep holes along the old river channel or in old lake basins. They remain in these holes or lake basins through the winter.

Big Rivers

Walleyes in big rivers begin their upstream spawning migration long before those in nearby lakes. In the North, the lakes are still ice-bound. As the walleyes work their way upstream, they gather in staging areas along the main channel. These areas are relatively deep, usually 20 to 30 feet, and have fairly light current or none at all. Walleyes will not stage up in places where they would have to fight the current to hold their position.

As spring progresses, the combination of lengthening days, warming water and increasing flow draws walleyes closer to

Tailwater eddies alongside the main current draw big-river walleyes before and after spawning and in fall.

their spawning grounds. Most big rivers have a series of dams that control the flow. When the gates of a dam are closed, they block the walleyes' upstream movement. Large numbers of fish gather in the tailwaters, awaiting the right conditions for spawning. They spawn on rocky shore- lines, particularly those with moderate current.

Not all walleyes spawn in the tailwaters. Many stop short on their upstream migration, selecting rocky, current-swept banks as much as several miles downstream from the dam. If the river is high enough to spill over its banks, walleyes spawn in flooded timber, brush or marsh grass.

Females begin moving downstream shortly after spawning. Some males remain in the spawning area up to two more weeks. On their way downstream, males and females gath- er in areas where current continually sweeps food past them. Holding in these areas enables them to feed without wasting energy.

After about two weeks of heavy feeding, walleyes regain their strength and begin to move toward summer habitat. As in spring, they are drawn to areas where food is plenti- ful. Water temperature has little influence on their move- ments because current mixes the water and keeps the tem- perature nearly uniform.

During the summer, walleyes hold near rocky points, wing- dams, and other current breaks in the main channel. These areas attract shiners and other baitfish. Some walleyes also hold in cuts leading into shallow backwaters. If baitfish are abundant, you can sometimes find walleyes in backwaters that would otherwise be too warm or weedy.

If the river widens out into lake-like habitat, look for walleyes around sunken islands, on long shoreline points or on other structure similar to that found in natural lakes.

In fall, river water cools evenly, unlike the water in a lake. As a result, river walleyes are not drawn into the shallows as much as lake walleyes. Usually, they stay in the same places they were in summer, until the water temperature drops into the 50s. Then they gradually begin to move upstream.

How far upstream walleyes go depends mainly on the depth of the main channel. If they can find depths of 30 feet or more, they will swim all the way to the dam and spend the winter in the tailwaters area. If not, they will hold in deep areas of the river channel several miles downstream.

Medium-Sized Rivers

Many medium-sized rivers have permanent walleye populations; others hold walleyes only in spring when fish from a connecting lake or big river move in to spawn.

During their upstream migration, walleyes concentrate in deep pools along outside bends, and in eddies. Some hold in deep spots in the main channel, if there are enough deep pockets or boulders to break the current.

Walleyes gradually work their way upstream until the water becomes too shallow or they encounter an impassible rapids. If there is a deep pool just downstream from the barrier, many walleyes will gather there to await spawning time.

Males start to congregate in the spawning area a week or more before the females. Spawning begins a few days after the females arrive. Some walleyes may spawn in the riffle area at the upper end of a pool; others along rubble shorelines just downstream from the barrier. Spawning areas usually have light to moderate current. Unless the water clarity is extremely low, almost all spawning takes place at night.

After spawning, females immediately begin working their way downstream; males remain near the spawning area for another week or two. On their way down the river, walleyes gather in washout holes along outside bends, and in deep pools and eddies. They feed heavily on current-brushed points and sandbars adjacent to the deep holding areas.

Walleyes that live in connecting waters continue to work their way downstream, then scatter to their summer habitat. Walleyes that live in the river stay in the post-spawn locations through the summer. If the river lacks deep holding areas, look for walleyes in pockets below log jams, around fallen trees or in other areas that offer shade.

In early fall, walleyes move somewhat shallower, but remain in the same general area where they spent the summer.

Fallen trees, especially those along deep banks, draw walleyes in summer on medium-sized rivers. The limbs and branches slow the current.

They feed heavily until the water temperature drops into the low 40s. Then, they begin to congregate in deep holes, especially those in long, shallow reaches of the river. They spend the entire winter in these holes and feed sporadically on nearby flats.

3

BASIC WALLEYE-FISHING
TECHNIQUES

Getting Started

You can greatly improve your odds of a successful walleye-fishing trip by doing a little homework in advance. A surprising amount of helpful information is available from state or provincial fisheries managers, conservation officers, tackle-shop operators and resort owners.

If you plan to fish a particular lake, ask about peak fishing times and try to schedule your trip accordingly. Find out if

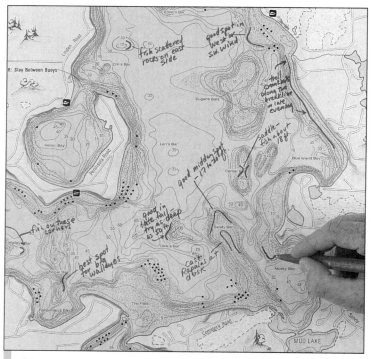

CONTOUR MAPS marked with the best walleye spots can be extremely valuable when fishing a strange lake. Instead of spending hours searching for a good spot, you can spend your time fishing. If you know someone who fishes the lake frequently, inquire about the possibility of sending you a marked map. If you cannot obtain a map in advance, buy one at a local tackle shop and ask the proprietor to mark some good walleye spots.

your contact is a fisherman. If so, inquire about the best baits and lures, the most effective fishing methods and when the walleyes are most likely to bite. Ask about depths where the fish are normally caught, the best types of structure and the most productive area of the lake.

Nobody can predict exactly when walleyes in a given body of water will bite, so there is always the chance that fishing will be slow despite all the information you have collected. To be on the safe side, line up a few backup waters in the same vicinity. A good selection of backups might include a shallow, murky lake in case of a cold front or calm, clear weather; a deep lake in case the season is more advanced than you had planned; and a small lake or river in case of windy weather. A river would also be a good choice following a cold front.

To avoid problems once you get to the lake, inspect your rods and reels before you leave home. Fill your reels with fresh line and carry extra spools with line of different weights. Check your tackle box to be sure that you have a good supply of terminal tackle and the right lures. Replace any rusty lure hooks and sharpen any dull ones. Failure to check any of these items could cost you a trophy walleye.

The best insurance against a disastrous trip is to hire a good guide for at least one day. If possible, talk to anglers who have fished the area before and can recommend a good guide. In a day of fishing, a competent guide can show you the best spots and fishing methods. This information will prove invaluable when you begin to fish on your own.

GATHERING INFORMATION

•*Public access maps* show the location of public fishing waters and boat-launching facilities. Many state or provincial natural-resources agencies provide these maps at no charge.

•*Regional fishing publications* reveal the location of prime walleye waters. Some provide information on acreage, depth and clarity of the water as well as data on walleye size and abundance.

•*Internet websites* maintained by state fish and game departments provide a wealth of fishing information on specific bodies of water.

How to Select Good Walleye Waters

North America has over 100 million acres of walleye water, so you should have no problem finding a place to fish. But many waters, especially those near population centers, are heavily fished, so the walleyes run on the small side.

If you are content with a mess of eating-size walleyes, you can easily get information on these well-known waters by inquiring at almost any bait shop or tackle store. For bigger walleyes, you will have a better chance in a more remote area. But gathering information on lesser-known waters is considerably more difficult.

Knowledgeable anglers are understandably tight-lipped when it comes to revealing their favorite walleye waters. If you cannot find a good fisherman willing to share his secrets, you can gather information from the following sources:

FISHING-CONTEST RESULTS. Certain waters annually produce surprising numbers of contest winners. If a lake or river never shows up in contest results, chances are it holds few big walleyes. Contest results may also provide information on the best baits and lures and the best times to fish.

LAKE SURVEYS. Many natural-resources agencies conduct lake surveys to provide information for fish management. If current information is available and you know how to analyze it, you can uncover some secret walleye waters of your own. Survey reports usually contain the following:

Fish-population data. Survey crews generally sample walleye populations using nets or electrofishing gear. These sampling devices cannot determine how many walleyes there

TEST NETTING gives natural-resources agencies a measure of the fish population in a body of water. Gill nets (above) catch fish by snaring them around the gills when they try to swim through the mesh. Most gill nets are designed to catch small to medium-sized fish because they are the ones most important to the future of the fishery. The gill nets used for sampling do not have mesh large enough to catch big walleyes.

are in a lake or river, but they provide an index of relative abundance. In other words, they give you an idea of the density of the walleye population compared to that in other waters sampled in similar fashion.

Population data from prior years can serve as an indicator of current walleye abundance. For instance, a strong year-class of age-two walleyes in test netting conducted one to two years ago means that the present fishing is probably good. Once the young fish reach two years old, they have escaped the most serious threats. At a typical growth rate, they will reach catchable size at three to four years of age.

Another important thing you can learn from studying fish-population data is the abundance of baitfish. A lake with an extremely high perch crop, for example, will usually have poor fishing despite a healthy walleye population.

Average depth. This is an important consideration when choosing a lake for fishing in early spring. A shallow lake warms more quickly than a deep one, so the walleyes begin to bite sooner. In fall, a shallow lake cools more quickly, so the turnover is earlier and walleyes may be harder to find than in a deeper lake that is still stratified.

Maximum depth is not a good indicator of how quickly a lake will warm. If a lake has one deep hole, but the rest of the basin is shallow, it may warm earlier than a lake where the maximum depth is not as great.

Clarity. Biologists measure water clarity by lowering an 8-inch black-and-white disc, called a Secchi disc, into the water until it is no longer visible.

The Secchi disc measurement gives you an indication of the time of day when fishing will be best. If the reading is a foot or less, chances are walleyes will feed intermittently from midmorning through midafternoon. If the reading is 10 feet or more, walleyes may feed only at night. Your best choice is a lake where the reading is between 3 and 8 feet. Here walleyes feed heavily around dusk and dawn with occasional feeding periods during the day.

Thermocline. Whether or not a lake has a thermocline, and the depth at which the thermocline is located, can play an important role in your walleye-fishing strategy.

Most shallow, windswept lakes do not form a thermocline. Walleyes may be as shallow as 5 feet or as deep as 30 feet, depending on light conditions and location of the forage.

Deeper lakes generally form a thermocline in summer. The walleye's preferred temperature zone is usually near the upper limit of the thermocline, so walleyes spend most of their time around that depth. As a result, summertime walleyes are usually easier to find in a deep lake than in a shallow one.

Oxygen. Survey reports often list dissolved oxygen levels at intervals from surface to bottom. Walleyes need a level of at least 4 parts per million to be comfortable (page 44). The oxygen readings will not tell you where to fish, but they will tell you where not to fish.

Boat traffic. Most survey reports mention the amount of boat traffic and other types of recreation that could interfere with fishing. In lakes or rivers where walleyes spend a good deal of their time at depths of 15 feet or less, heavy boat traffic will cause walleyes to stop biting and move to deeper water. So even though there is a good population of walleyes, you may have difficulty catching them, especially on weekends. On these waters, walleyes usually bite best early in the morning, before the traffic starts.

STOCKING RECORDS. Records kept by natural resources agencies can give an indication of the size of the existing walleye population. If the lake was stocked heavily several years earlier, it may hold good numbers of walleyes. However, these records can be misleading because the survival of young fish, especially fry, is very uncertain.

CONTOUR MAPS. Hydrographic maps are available for most important fishing waters. They tell you a great deal about the walleye-fishing potential of these waters, if you know what to look for. The examples on pages 88-89 show you how to evaluate that potential based on the shape of the lake basin. All of the examples show typical walleye location in summer, after the thermocline has formed.

HOW TO SELECT A LAKE ON THE BASIS OF STRUCTURE

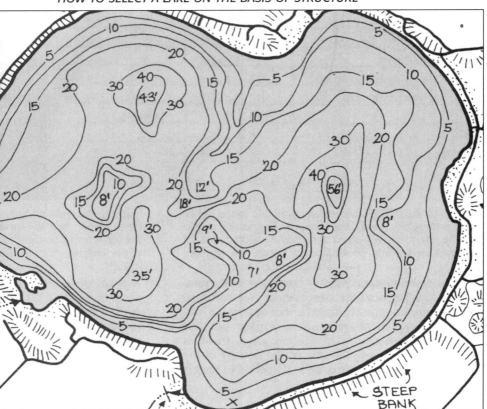

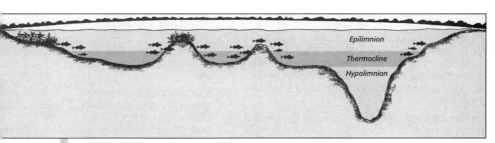

PRIME walleye lakes generally have a moderate amount of structure such as points, irregular breaklines, and offshore reefs and sunken islands (top). The offshore structure should top off in the thermocline or above it (bottom) and should be linked to other walleye structure rather than isolated by deep water.

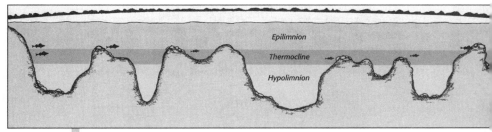

TOO MUCH STRUCTURE can make walleye fishing difficult, even if the lake has a good population. Often, you can find a walleye or two on a seemingly good spot, but seldom a big school. Walleyes are not as likely to be concentrated as in the lake at the left because they have many more good spots to choose from.

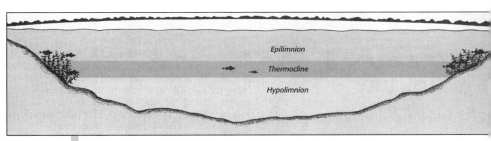

LACK OF STRUCTURE can also make walleye fishing tough. A lake may be teeming with walleyes, but they can be hard to find if there is no structure to concentrate them. In this bowl-shaped lake, some of the walleyes suspend in the thermocline; others scatter along the shoreline, in the weeds or along the weedline.

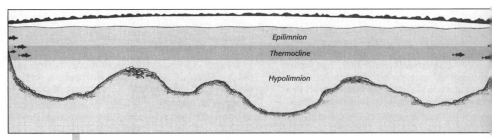

DEEP STRUCTURE has little value to walleyes during the summer. The humps and reefs in this lake top off at 30 to 40 feet, but the thermocline ends at 25 feet. Below the thermocline, the water is too cold and may lack oxygen, so walleyes will most likely be scattered along the shoreline or suspended in the thermocline.

Recognizing Good Walleye Structure

One of the big mysteries of walleye fishing is why certain spots consistently hold fish, but other seemingly identical spots do not. The answer lies in some slight variation that may not be noticeable to a fisherman but makes a big difference to a walleye.

Learning to evaluate structure quickly and recognize these slight variations is the key to walleye-fishing success. A

SCOUT potential walleye structure by watching your depth finder while motoring at high speed. This enables you to cover a lot of water quickly. Be sure your transducer is adjusted for high-speed reading.

skillful presentation will do you no good if you cannot locate the fish.

Before you begin your search for productive walleye structure, you must understand the seasonal movements of walleyes in the type of water you are fishing. Study the section, "Where to Find Walleyes through the Seasons" (page 64), to get an idea of the kind of structure that will hold walleyes in each season. Then, fine-tune your selection process by evaluating the following:

BOTTOM TYPE. Walleyes generally prefer a firm bottom, but which bottom material is the best varies in different waters. As a rule, walleyes look for something different from the rest of their surroundings. In a lake where the bottom is mainly sand, for instance, rocky reefs draw large numbers of walleyes. But in a rocky lake, sandy, weed-covered sunken islands are often better than rocky reefs.

In waters with large expanses of mucky bottom, a patch of sand, gravel or rock is usually a prime walleye spot, even if there is no change in depth.

MINIMUM DEPTH. The depth at which a piece of structure tops off (illustration on page 92) can determine whether or not it holds walleyes. Because they prefer to feed on a relatively flat shelf rather than a drop-off, they spend a good deal of time on top of the structure. In a stratified lake, they select structure that tops off in the zone where the water temperature is most comfortable.

DEPTH OF NEARBY WATER. Walleyes will seldom cross a wide expanse of deep water to reach an isolated piece of structure. They prefer to follow migration routes in their normal depth range. As a result, you would be more likely to find walleyes on an offshore reef connected to another reef by a saddle than on an offshore reef surrounded on all sides by deep water.

Structure connected to the shoreline is generally the best choice in spring. After spawning, walleyes remain near shore, where the temperature is warmest. But when inshore temperatures rise to the low 60s, many of them move to offshore structure that offers easy access to the depths. If there is no offshore structure, walleyes select areas of the shoreline break adjacent to deep water.

DEGREE OF SLOPE. Early in the year, walleyes seek out structure that slopes very gradually (illustration below). Because they remain in relatively shallow water all day, they have no need for a sharp drop-off. By midsummer, most of them have moved to structure with a more pronounced slope. The sharper drop-off makes it easy to move deeper when the sun comes up. In late fall, they move to structure with an even steeper slope. This way, they can grab a quick meal in the shallows, then quickly retreat to warmer water in the depths.

In shallow lakes that lack noticeable structure, walleyes relate to subtle depth changes. A sunken island that rises gradually to a height of 2 feet above the surrounding bottom may attract large numbers of fish. In a lake with more

HOW DEPTH AND SLOPE OF STRUCTURE AFFECT SEASONAL WALLEYE LOCATION

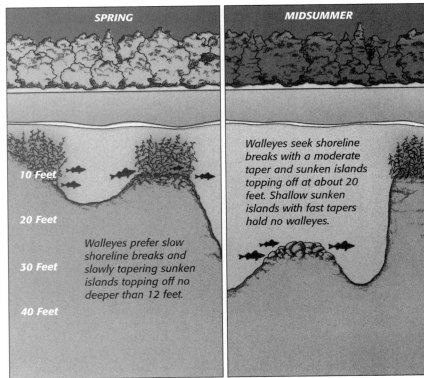

SPRING

10 Feet

20 Feet

Walleyes prefer slow shoreline breaks and slowly tapering sunken islands topping off no deeper than 12 feet.

30 Feet

40 Feet

MIDSUMMER

Walleyes seek shoreline breaks with a moderate taper and sunken islands topping off at about 20 feet. Shallow sunken islands with fast tapers hold no walleyes.

structure, they would probably not relate to such a minor depth change.

BREAKLINE CONFIGURATION. Structure that has an irregular breakline with numerous points and inside turns will generally hold more walleyes than structure that has a straight breakline.

SIZE. All other factors being equal, a large piece of structure is more likely to hold walleyes than a small one. Walleyes would soon drive the baitfish off a small reef, exhausting the food supply. But on a big reef, baitfish that escape would move a short distance away, then gradually filter back.

HIGH-PERCENTAGE WALLEYE STRUCTURE

•*Big reefs* that slope gradually into deep water are especially productive in summer. Reefs with firm bottoms and cover such as rocks or scattered weed clumps hold more walleyes than soft-bottomed humps with no cover.

•*Rock piles* on an otherwise smooth bottom draw walleyes all year. Algae on the rocks attracts crustaceans and baitfish, which in turn draw walleyes. Rocks also provide shade and give the walleyes something to relate to.

•*Points and inside turns* along a shoreline break are consistent walleye producers, particularly

LATE FALL

Walleyes seek sharp shoreline breaks leading to deep water and fast-tapering sunken islands that top off at 30 to 50 feet.

LOOK for structure with different slopes and minimum depths in different seasons. In a typical stratified mesotrophic lake, the type of structure preferred by walleyes in different seasons is shown to the left.

in spring. The best breaklines have a wide, shallow feeding shelf extending from shore.

•*Saddles* linking one piece of structure to another concentrate walleyes. A saddle serves as an underwater highway, so walleyes following this shoreline break would be naturally drawn to the offshore hump.

•*Long fingers* projecting from any type of structure also concentrate walleyes. They generally hold just off the tip, then use the finger as a path when moving into shallower water to feed.

•*Shaded structure* holds walleyes on bright days. Submerged weeds several feet high will cast a significant shadow. Fishing along a breakline is usually best where there is a shadow on the deep side of the weeds.

LOW-PERCENTAGE WALLEYE STRUCTURE

•*Small humps* that drop rapidly into deep water generally draw few walleyes. The small flat surface on top does not make a good feeding shelf and the sheer sides do not provide a comfortable resting area.

•*Sand flats* with no weeds, rocks or other cover seldom hold walleyes. The sterile sand bottom produces little if any invertebrate life. As a result, these flats draw few baitfish.

•*Short-lipped points* are less likely to hold walleyes than points that project a long distance. Because these points usually lack a shallow feeding shelf, walleyes have little reason to use them.

•*Long, narrow points* may lack a feeding shelf, even though they project a long distance. Points that rise rapidly from deep water, then immediately plunge back down usually hold few walleyes.

•*Sheer drop-offs* rarely attract walleyes, even in late fall when the fish prefer sharp-tapering structure. Walleyes often rest with their fins touching bottom, an impossibility along an underwater cliff.

•*Straight breaklines* may have a few walleyes, but the fish are seldom as concentrated as on the points and inside turns of an irregular breakline. But in bowl-shaped lakes, a straight breakline may be the only choice.

Boat Control

The importance of precise boat control in walleye fishing cannot be overemphasized. Walleyes often form tight schools, sometimes no more than a few feet across. Unless you can position your boat to work an exact spot, you will not catch walleyes consistently.

Another reason for precise boat control: all walleyes along a given piece of structure are likely to be at a similar depth.

HOW TO BACKTROLL ALONG AN IRREGULAR BREAKLINE

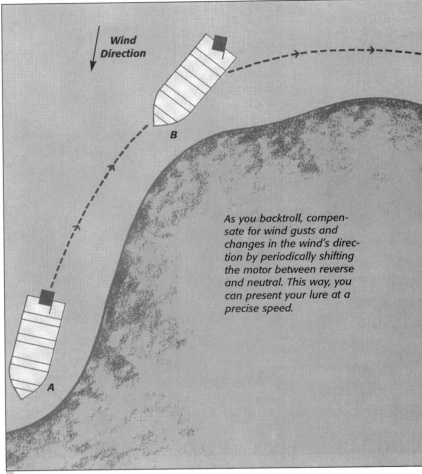

Wind Direction

B

As you backtroll, compensate for wind gusts and changes in the wind's direction by periodically shifting the motor between reverse and neutral. This way, you can present your lure at a precise speed.

A

POINT the transom into the wind and begin trolling in reverse. Watch your flasher closely, and when the depth changes, steer in the appropriate direction. In the above example, the angler is trolling from A to D.

If you attempt to follow a specific contour, but your boat continually weaves from deep to shallow water, your bait will be in the fish zone only a small fraction of the time.

By mastering the following boat-control techniques, you can greatly improve your fishing success.

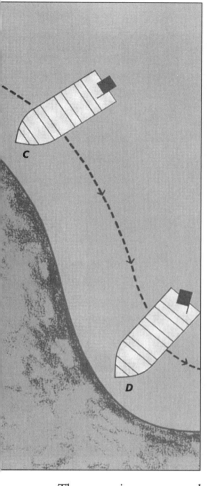

BACKTROLLING. The term *backtrolling* means trolling transom-first rather than bow-first. Backtrolling is a technique every walleye angler should learn. It offers the following advantages over forward trolling:

•You can troll much more slowly because the transom has more water resistance than the bow. In addition, most outboard motors are geared lower in reverse than in forward, so they troll more slowly at the same RPMs.

•A boat moving in reverse is easier to control and less likely to be blown off course than one moving forward. The principle is much the same in a front-wheel-drive automobile. Because the weight and power are at the leading end, it hugs the road better and is less affected by crosswinds than an automobile with rear-wheel drive.

•Because the lines trail toward the bow rather than the stern, fishermen in the front seats will not get their lines tangled in the motor.

The most important rule of backtrolling is to move against the wind. If you backtroll with the wind, your bow will swing to the side and you will not be able to control the boat's direction. In most cases, the wind will be at an angle to the breakline, so you will not be able to troll directly into the wind and still follow the contour. But you can angle the transom into the wind and still maintain good control.

In a strong wind, you will need quite a bit of power to move the boat against the waves. In addition, you may need splash guards (photo on page 95) to prevent waves from breaking over the transom.

Most anglers prefer an outboard with a tiller handle for back-trolling. A tiller allows you to steer and operate the throttle with one hand while fishing with the other. If your outboard has power trim, you can slow your backtrolling speed by trimming the motor up. If the wind is light, a transom-mounted electric trolling motor works better than an outboard. It enables you to troll more quietly and move more slowly. And there are no exhaust fumes to blow into your face.

DRIFTING. This technique is most valuable in the following situations:

•*On big water* where backtrolling would be impossible because of heavy wave action.

•*In shallow water* where trolling over the fish would spook them.

•*At the end of a backtrolling run,* to fish your way back to the starting point for another run.

To completely cover a piece of structure such as a reef or flat, make parallel drifts over it (diagram on opposite page). Start each drift at a different spot so you are always fishing new water.

When drifting along a breakline after a backtrolling run, use your outboard or trolling motor to keep the boat on course. If you simply let the wind blow the boat, you will not follow the breakline, unless the wind happens to be blowing exactly parallel to it.

Drifting with the current is a widely used technique in rivers. Use a motor to control your drift, just as you would in a lake.

In a strong wind, you may have trouble presenting your lure or bait slowly enough to catch walleyes. A drift sock (page 23) will slow your drift by as much as 90 percent. Other tricks for controlling your boat in the wind include filling your live well with water and positioning the heaviest fisherman in the bow seat. The extra weight in the front will keep the bow from swinging as much.

An outboard motor, even though it is not running, will help keep the boat drifting crosswise to the wind. Simply steer as you would if the motor were running and let the

HOW TO WORK A REEF BY DRIFTING

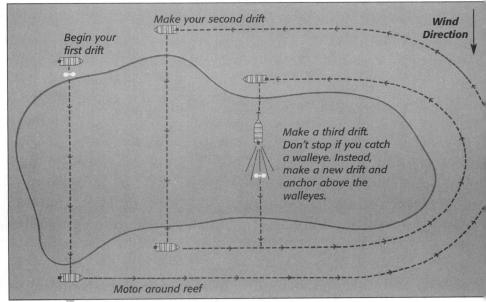

LOCATE walleyes on a reef by making a series of parallel drifts across the reef. By casting to each side of your drift path, you can cover a swath at least 100 feet wide on each drift. When you catch a walleye, mark the spot. Instead of stopping to work the area, complete your drift and motor back around the reef. Anchor your boat far enough upwind of your marker so you do not disturb the walleyes, then fan-cast the area.

rudder control your drift. Keeping the boat crosswise is especially important with two or more fishermen. It allows you to cover a wider swath and keeps the lines from tangling.

SLIPPING. This is another technique for slowing the speed of your drift in a strong wind or in fast current. One method of slipping is to point the bow into the wind or current and run the outboard in forward gear. Adjust your throttle so the boat drifts at the desired speed. You can easily move from one side to the other by pointing the bow slightly in the desired direction.

Another method is to turn your transom into the wind or current, then backtroll. The principle is exactly the same, but some fishermen feel they have more control this way.

If you locate a school of walleyes, you can use the slipping technique to hover over them. Simply open the throttle until the boat remains stationary.

FORWARD TROLLING. The technique of forward trolling with an outboard requires little explanation, but forward trolling with a bow-mounted electric motor is more complicated.

Using a bow-mount for forward trolling is equivalent to using an outboard for backtrolling. You have good control because the boat is powered from the leading end. The principles of operating a bow-mount are very similar to those discussed for backtrolling, but there are a few important differences.

On most boats, the depth-finder transducer is mounted on the lower edge of the transom. This works well for backtrolling because you get a depth reading directly below your motor, enabling you to adjust your course immediately as the depth changes. When forward trolling with a bow-mounted motor, however, the transom-mounted transducer may read a depth different from that below the motor. This prevents you from making the proper course adjustments, so you spend too much time fishing at the wrong depth. The best solution is to mount a transducer on the lower unit of your bow-mounted motor.

One drawback to forward trolling with a bow-mount is that your line tends to catch on the outboard, especially when a crosswind causes the line to angle under the boat. When you get a bite, you may have to run to the back of the boat to free the line from the outboard before setting the hook.

ANCHORING. This is the ultimate method of boat control because you can hold your boat in the exact position you want. Trolling and drifting are the best ways to locate walleyes, but once you find a school, you can work it more effectively by anchoring. And anchoring reduces the chance of spooking the fish.

To anchor securely, you must have a rope that is long enough and an anchor that is heavy enough and designed to bite into the bottom. If your anchor slips, it may drag through a school of walleyes and scatter them.

When fishing in a strong wind or fast current, tie your anchor rope to the bow. If you tie it to the stern, water may come over the transom. If you tie it to the side, water may slosh over the gunwale, and because the wind pushes against such a large area of the boat, the anchor may not hold. When anchored from the bow, the boat will ride better on the waves and is less likely to take on water.

Before anchoring, estimate how much rope you will need to hold the boat, then drop anchor at least that far upwind or upstream of the desired boat position. In strong wind or current, you may have to allow for some slippage before the anchor catches.

With the rope tied to the bow, even a slight wind or light current will cause the boat to swing back and forth. You can increase or decrease the amount of swing by using an electric motor. And you can hold the boat to one side or the other by turning your outboard to take advantage of the rudder. If you do not want the boat to swing, drop another anchor at the stern and leave only a small amount of slack.

To anchor sideways, simply turn the boat at a right angle to the wind or current, then drop two anchors simultaneously, one from the bow and the other from the stern. This way, the boat cannot swing from side to side and each angler has an equal chance of reaching the fish. Never anchor from the side in a strong wind or current because the boat could easily capsize.

QUICK TIP: If you want to cover a large area from an anchored postion, attach the anchor to the bow. This way, the boat will swing from side to side, allowing you to cast to a larger area than if the boat did not swing.

Live Bait

Fishing surveys show that live bait accounts for at least two-thirds of all walleyes caught on hook and line. Even the staunchest artificial-lure advocates switch to live bait or add live bait to their lures when walleye fishing really gets tough.

The best live baits for walleyes include minnows and other small fish, nightcrawlers and leeches. There are times when other kinds of baits, such as waterdogs and frogs, will also produce. But they seldom work better, and are usually less effective. Your choice of live bait depends mainly on availability and the time of year.

Some baits are not available year-round. Leeches, for example, cannot be caught in early spring because they are not active enough to swim into traps. Many bait shops do not carry shiner minnows in summer. At typical summer water temperatures, they are difficult to keep alive in a bait dealer's tank or in your minnow bucket.

Walleyes favor different types of bait in different seasons. Nightcrawlers rank among the best summertime baits, but in most waters, they do not work well in early spring. Minnows are a good choice in spring and again in fall, but may not be as effective in summer.

At times, the species of minnow can make a big difference. In spring, shiners often produce when nothing else will. But in fall, other minnows like redtail chubs may outfish shiners. Different types of minnows are effective in different waters, so it pays to ask your bait dealer what works best in the body of water you plan to fish.

Many anglers consider ribbon leeches to be the best all-around walleye bait. They swim enticingly at water temperatures of 50°F or higher. But leeches are not a good choice in cold water because they often curl around the hook, forming a useless ball.

Whatever the bait you choose, make sure that it is lively. When walleyes are really biting, you can often get by with

a dead minnow or chewed-up nightcrawler, but a struggling minnow or squirming crawler will normally catch many more fish.

Slip-Sinker Fishing

Slow-trolling with slip-sinker rigs probably accounts for more walleyes than any other technique. It is simple yet extremely effective, enabling you to present live bait so it stays lively and appears natural. Because the line slides freely through the sinker, a walleye feels no resistance when it grabs the bait and swims off. With a fixed sinker, a walleye may feel the tension and let go.

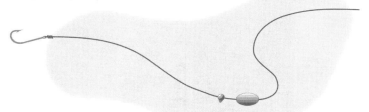

Slip-sinker rigs are versatile. They work well for walleyes hugging the bottom or suspended well above it. They can be fished over any bottom material or through dense weeds. And they are effective at depths from less than 10 feet to over 50.

There are many variations of the basic slip-sinker rig, each intended for a slightly different fishing purpose. The variations will be shown in the chapter on techniques for special situations (page 130).

You can purchase pretied slip-sinker rigs, but many anglers prefer to make their own to suit their style of fishing. When buying or assembling a slip-sinker rig, consider the following:

TYPE OF SINKER. The size of your sinker depends mainly on the water depth. As a general rule, you will need about 1/8 ounce of weight for every 10 feet of depth. At a depth of 20 feet, for instance, you would need a 1/4-ounce sinker. But you may have to use more weight when fishing in wind or current.

In clear water, you may have to use a sinker lighter than normal and let out more line to prevent spooking the fish.

Sinker style is dictated by the type of bottom. On a clean, smooth bottom, any sinker will do as long as the line slips through freely. On a weedy bottom, a cone sinker works best because it will not catch vegetation. On a rocky bottom, a snag-resistant sinker is the best choice. Many anglers prefer removable sinkers so they can switch weights without untying the rig.

TYPE OF HOOK. The hook should be small enough that a walleye can swim off and swallow the bait without detecting anything unusual. Select a hook with an extremely sharp point, a relatively short shank and either a straight or turned-up eye. Most anglers prefer a size 6 to 8 hook for leeches and nightcrawlers; size 2 to 4 for minnows. You may need a larger hook for big minnows.

To keep your bait above a snaggy bottom or to reach suspended walleyes, use a hook with styrofoam, cork or hollow plastic molded around the shank for flotation. Called floating jig heads, these hooks usually have a fluorescent-colored body. You can also float your hook by attaching a small cork or styrofoam ball to the leader.

You can add color to your slip-sinker rig without using a floating jig head by tying a small piece of fluorescent yarn to your hook. Some fishermen add a spinner blade ahead of the hook. At times, the extra color or flash makes a big difference.

TYPE OF LEADER. When walleyes are near bottom, there is no need for a long leader. An 18- to 36-inch leader works well in this situation. But when the fish are suspended, you may need a leader over 10 feet long.

Use a light, low-visibility mono leader, especially when fishing in clear water. Many commercial rigs have leaders that are much too heavy. Walleyes are more likely to see a heavy leader, so you will get fewer bites. A 6-pound leader is adequate in most situations, but you may need an 8- to 10-pound leader on a snaggy bottom. In extremely clear water or when the walleyes are sluggish, a 4-pound leader may improve your success.

TYPE OF STOP. To prevent the sinker from sliding down to the hook, you will need a stop. The simplest stop is a split-shot pinched onto the line at the desired position. But if the sinker snags, the split-shot may slip and fray your line. The most common stop is a barrel swivel. A swivel allows you to use a leader that is lighter than your main line. Then, if the hook becomes snagged, you can break it off without losing your entire rig.

A handy stop which enables you to adjust your leader length is a slip-bobber knot with a bead to keep the knot from slipping through the sinker. Or use only the bead and loop the line around it. To adjust the leader, loosen the loop and move the bead.

To troll a slip-sinker rig effectively, you must master the basics of boat control. To detect pickups, which are often extremely subtle, keep your line as short as possible. This means you must move the boat very slowly. And once you locate the walleyes, you must be able to follow the contour so you stay at the precise depth. If you move your bait too fast or wander back and forth across the structure, you will catch few walleyes.

You can also cast and retrieve a slip-sinker rig from an anchored boat or from shore. Many fishermen troll until they locate some walleyes, then anchor away from them and cast into the school. This technique works well in shallow water where continually trolling over the fish would spook them.

QUICK TIP: For slip-sinker fishing, hook a minnow through the lips; a night-crawler through the head or on a harness; a leech through the sucker or the neck, which has tough skin, making it hard for panfish to steal the bait; a frog or waterdog through the lips. Use a stinger hook with a waterdog.

Effective slip-sinker fishing requires a sensitive rod with a flexible tip. Most experts use a medium-action graphite rod from 6½ to 7½ feet long. A flexible tip offers less resistance than a stiff one should you fail to release the line when a walleye swims off with the bait.

Keep your spinning reel filled with line. When a walleye moves with the bait, line will flow easily from the spool. If the spool is not filled, the line may catch and cause the fish to drop the bait.

HOW TO TROLL WITH A SLIP-SINKER RIG

•*Lower* the rig until the sinker touches bottom. Let out no more line than necessary; if you let out too much, you will have trouble feeling bites. Continually adjust the amount of line as the depth changes.

•*Troll* with your bail open, holding the line with your index finger. If you feel resistance, pull back very gently with your rod tip. A shake or any other sign of life indicates a fish; a dead pull is probably a stick or weed.

• *Drop* the line off your index finger immediately when you determine that you have a bite (above). If you fail to release the line in time, the fish will detect too much resistance and let go of your bait.

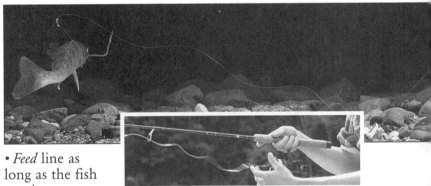

• *Feed* line as long as the fish continues to run. If you are right-handed, use your left hand to strip line from the reel (above). This is a precaution to assure that the line does not catch on the spool.

• *Reel rapidly* to take up slack once the fish stops running. Continue reeling until you feel weight. You may have to reel up more line than you think; a walleye may double back rather than move straight away.

• *Set the hook* with a sharp snap of the wrists when you feel the weight of the fish. Attempting to set the hook before all of the slack is removed is the most common mistake in slip-sinker fishing.

Fishing with Spinner-Live Bait Combinations

Spinner-live bait rigs have ranked among the top walleye baits for decades, and they remain just as effective today. Vibration and flash from the spinner blade attract a walleye's attention. Spinner-live bait rigs work best in low-clarity water, but will catch walleyes anywhere.

The amount of vibration a spinner produces depends on the style and size of blade. A Colorado blade turns at about a 50-degree angle to the shaft; an Indiana blade, about 40 degrees; and a willow-leaf blade, about 25 degrees. The greater the angle and the larger the blade, the stronger the beat.

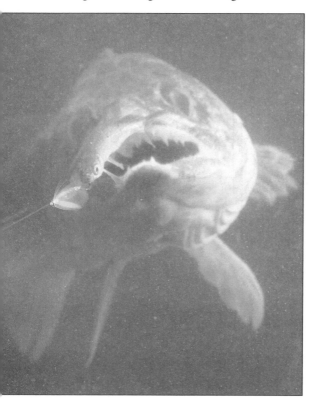

Blades that produce a strong beat work well in low-clarity water or at night because walleyes can detect the vibration with their lateral-line sense even if they cannot see the spinner. In this situation, a large Colorado blade would most likely be the best choice. But in clearer water, walleyes seem to prefer a less intense vibration, so a small willow-leaf blade may be more effective.

BASIC SPINNER-LIVE BAIT RIGS

SPINNERS include: (1) single-hook rigs, such as the Northland Rainbow Spinner; (2) triple-hook rigs, such as the Northland String'r Hook Harness; (3) floating rigs, such as the Northland Float'n Spin Harness; and (4) weight-forward spinners, such as the Storm Hot'N Tot Pygmy.

Colorado blades work well in spring, when walleyes prefer a slow-moving bait. Because these blades have more water resistance than others, they require less speed to make them spin. Willow-leaf blades are effective in summer and early fall, when walleyes are more willing to chase fast-moving baits. These blades have the least water resistance and require the most speed to make them turn. Indiana blades have intermediate qualities, making them a good all-season choice.

Spinners can be used in combination with almost any type of live bait, but minnows, nightcrawlers and leeches are most popular.

Spinner-live bait rigs are usually fished by trolling or drifting along a breakline. But they also work well for fishing over weedtops. The spinning blade functions as a weed-guard and provides enough lift to keep the rig skimming over the vegetation.

Weight-forward spinners and spinnerbaits have lead bodies, so they work well for casting. They are effective for suspended walleyes because you can count them down to a precise depth and retrieve them at that level. Spinnerbaits can be retrieved through dense vegetation. The wire arms deflect weeds, and keep them from fouling the hook.

Most spinners, except weight-forward types and spinnerbaits, require a sinker to reach the desired depth. Many fishermen use a bead-chain or keel sinker to prevent line twist, but some prefer a slip sinker so they can feed line when a fish bites. When fishing over rocks, logs or brush, use some type of snag-resistant sinker.

Many spinner-live bait rigs come with a two- or three-hook harness. With the trailing hook in the tail of the bait, you can set the hook immediately when you feel a strike. You can also set immediately with a single hook, if you feel a hard strike. But if you feel only a gentle tug, drop your rod tip back, hesitate a few seconds to let the fish take the bait, then set the hook. A long rod, from 6$\frac{1}{2}$ to 7$\frac{1}{2}$ feet, enables you to drop the tip back farther and gives you a longer sweep for setting the hook.

QUICK TIP: Small blades in sizes 00 to 1 work well in cold or clear water; larger blades in sizes 2 to 4 are more effective in warm or low-clarity water or at night.

Fluorescent orange, red and chartreuse are the best blade colors for fishing in low-clarity water. Silver, copper, gold, brass, blue and green are better choices in clearer water.

Mono-leader type spinners should be tied with the lightest line practical, to avoid spooking the fish. Line from 8- to 10-pound test is usually adequate, but you may need 15-pound line in timber or brush.

Slip-Bobber Fishing

The idea of using a bobber for walleyes may draw a snicker from some anglers, but there are times when slip-bobber fishing will take more walleyes than any other technique.

Slip-bobber rigs work well in situations where walleyes are suspended at a specific depth or holding over a snaggy bottom. They are also effective when walleyes are not in the mood to feed. After a cold front, for instance, walleyes refuse to chase anything moving too rapidly, but may strike a bait dangling in front of them.

Because a slip-bobber rig seldom snags, you can use lighter line than with most other bait rigs. Six-pound-test mono is a good choice for most situations. Heavier line slides through the bobber more slowly and is more visible to the fish.

To set the depth, simply slide your bobber stop up the line the same distance that you want your bait to hang below the surface. The stop should slide freely so that it does not scuff your line when you want to change depth. But it should not be so loose that it slips while you reel in your line. You can buy a variety of bobber stops or make your own stop using a slip-bobber knot.

When you get a bite, wait a few seconds, then gently tighten your line until you feel weight. Failure to tighten the line at this point is the most common reason for losing fish. The bobber creates an angle between you and the walleye, so there will be slack line if you attempt to set the hook without performing this crucial step. A long, stiff rod is best for taking up slack and sinking the hook.

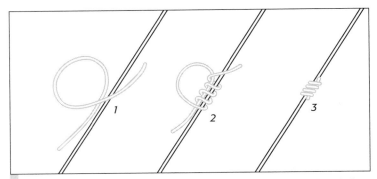

TIE a slip-bobber knot by (1) making a loop with a piece of braided dacron, then holding the loop alongside the mono. (2) Pass one end of the dacron through the loop and around the mono. Continue until three or four wraps are completed. (3) Snug up the knot and trim.

You can also improve your hooking percentage by waiting until the fish stops moving or begins to swim away from you. This gives you a better angle for setting the hook than if the fish were swimming toward you.

Fishing with a slip-bobber is relatively easy. Begin by making a lob-cast with a sidearm motion. If you snap your wrist, the hook may tangle around the bobber. Pay out line after the cast so that it can slip through the bobber freely. Watch carefully to be sure the line is slipping; if not, the rig is probably tangled. Continue paying out line. When the bait reaches the right depth, the knot will prevent the line from slipping any farther, causing the bobber to stand upright.

> QUICK TIP: For slip-bobber fishing, rig a leech by pushing a size 6 hook through the sucker end or the middle; a minnow with a size 4 hook through the back; a nightcrawler with a size 6 hook through the middle so both ends dangle free.

Other Bait-Fishing Rigs and Techniques

The rigs and techniques discussed on the previous live-bait pages will produce walleyes in most fishing situations. But there are times when less popular rigs and techniques work better. A good walleye fisherman should know how and when to use the following live-bait rigs:

SPLIT-SHOT RIGS work well in shallow water or when walleyes are spooky. A split-shot rig, which consists of one or more split-shots placed 1 to 3 feet up from the hook, lets the bait move naturally. And by using a minimum of weight and reeling slowly, you can keep the rig above a snaggy bottom.

BOTTOM-WALKER RIGS are effective when snags are a problem. The specially designed bottom-walking sinkers walk over obstructions with relatively few hang-ups. Try to hold the lead weight off bottom, so that only the wire leg touches.

WOLF-RIVER RIGS are most popular for river fishing, but will work anywhere. These rigs consist of a dropper on a three-way swivel. By design, the Wolf-River rig keeps the bait off bottom so fish can see it. The longer the dropper, the higher the bait will ride.

How to Keep Live Bait

Fresh, lively bait is a must in walleye fishing. There are times when a walleye will grab a dead minnow, a shriveled-up leech or a nightcrawler that is barely wiggling. But in almost every situation, a bait that swims or squirms naturally will catch more walleyes, and usually bigger ones.

Regardless of the type of bait, always keep it cool. Minnows use less oxygen when kept in cool water. Nightcrawlers in cool bedding stay firm and lively. Leeches can tolerate warm water, but will die if left in the sun in a shallow container. The following tips will help you keep your bait in good condition.

•*Place* a flow-through minnow bucket in your live well when moving from spot to spot or for overnight storage when your boat is out of the water. The large volume of water in the live well ensures that the minnows will not run short of oxygen.

•*Keep* a large quantity of minnows by placing them in a good-sized aerated bucket. An aerated bucket enables you to keep more minnows than you could in a flow-through or styrofoam bucket. The small aerator will operate for several days on a fully charged deep-cycle battery.

•*Store* nightcrawlers in commercial worm bedding, cover them with a damp towel and keep them refrigerated. The towel keeps the bedding moist. When fishing, keep a container of worms and bedding in a cooler along with a block of ice.

•*Pour* leeches from the small plastic containers into a styrofoam minnow bucket. A styrofoam bucket keeps them fresh for several days without a change of water. It also provides good insulation to protect the leeches from a rapid rise in temperature, which could kill them.

Artificial Lures

The complete walleye fisherman must be proficient with artificial lures as well as live bait. Although live bait accounts for the majority of walleyes caught by angling, there are times when artificials work better.

When walleyes are scattered, for instance, trolling or casting an artificial enables you to cover a lot of water quickly. Once you find a school and catch the aggressive fish, the action slows. But you may be able to catch a few more by switching to live bait.

Trolling an artificial lure is an excellent way to explore unfamiliar water. Watch your depth finder as you follow the structure. Look for points and inside turns on the breakline, areas of hard bottom and schools of fish. If you get a strike or notice a likely spot, toss out a marker so you can return later.

Artificial lures often work better than live bait in fast-moving or low-clarity water. Walleyes in current do not have much time to inspect their food. They learn to strike at any movement or flash. Walleyes in murky water may be able to see only a few inches, but they can detect the sound and vibration from an artificial lure.

Many anglers prefer artificials for night fishing. Walleyes can spot the silhouette of a lure against the surface more easily than they can see a bait hanging from a bobber or moving slowly along bottom. And artificials eliminate the problem of baiting your hook at night.

When walleyes are on a feeding binge, you can catch them more quickly with lures than with live bait. In the time it would take to remove your old minnow and hook on a fresh one, you can cast a lure and possibly catch another fish.

The following section will discuss artificial lures that can be used without live bait. Artificials that are normally tipped with bait are shown in the live-bait section (pages 102-113).

Fishing with Jigs

No other artificial lure will catch walleyes as consistently as a lead-head jig. A jig is a natural choice for walleyes because it is easy to keep on bottom, where the fish spend most of their time.

Among the most versatile of artificial lures, jigs can be fished in many different ways. You can cast from an anchored or drifting boat, jig vertically while drifting with

the wind or current, or troll slowly while bumping the jig along bottom. And you can fish a jig plain when walleyes are biting, or tip it with live bait when fishing is slow.

CASTING. The most widely used jig-fishing technique, casting works well in shallow water. When walleyes are in the shallows, drifting or trolling over them or even anchoring nearby will probably spook them. But you will not disturb them if you anchor at a distance and cast.

To work a shallow reef, for instance, anchor in deep water so the wind pushes you into position for casting to the desired area of the reef. If nothing bites in a few minutes, pull up the anchor and reposition in a different spot. Continue moving until you find the fish. Anchoring and casting also works well for fishing eddies, pools and pockets in rivers.

When walleyes are scattered along a breakline, let your boat drift just off the break and cast into the shallows. Use your electric motor or outboard to keep the boat drifting parallel to the breakline. If you catch a walleye, toss a marker and work the spot more thoroughly.

To catch walleyes suspended off bottom, count your jig down to a different depth after each cast, then begin your retrieve. When you get a strike, repeat the count on the next cast.

VERTICAL JIGGING. Use a jig heavy enough that you can keep your line nearly vertical. Bounce the jig along bottom while drifting with the wind or current, continually adjusting your line length as the depth changes. Keep your bail open and hold the line with your finger so you can easily let out a little more line when the water gets deeper. When it gets shallower, reel in the slack so the jig does not drag.

When walleyes are in deep water, vertical jigging generally works better than casting. Because of the greater line angle, you can hop the jig higher and give it more action. The extra action often triggers walleyes to strike, especially in low-clarity water.

Another advantage of jigging vertically: you can feel strikes more easily. Because you are using a minimum of line, stretch does not diminish the feel of a strike as much as it would with a longer line.

Vertical jigging is effective in lakes or rivers. In a lake, jig vertically while letting the wind push your boat over likely structure. In a river, let the boat drift with the current, keeping it at a likely depth.

JIG TROLLING. This technique combines vertical jigging with backtrolling. Lower your jig to bottom, then troll slowly in reverse while following a breakline or exploring a reef. Twitch the jig to hop it off bottom, then lower it back with a taut line. Continually adjust your line length as you would when jigging vertically.

The key to success in jig trolling is to move very slowly. If you troll too fast, your jig will lose contact with the bottom. And because you will have to let out more line, strikes will be harder to detect. For slower speed and better boat control, always troll against the wind.

With any of these techniques, the way you work your jig depends on the season and the mood of the walleyes. In spring and fall, when the water is cool, small hops generally work better than big ones. But in summer, larger hops often catch more fish. In late fall and winter, walleyes sometimes prefer a jig dragged slowly on bottom, with no hopping action. Because the walleyes' mood can change from day to day, it pays to vary your retrieve until you find the action that works best.

Jig fishing demands intense concentration and a sensitive touch. When a walleye grabs a jig, what you feel ranges from

HOW TO SELECT A JIG

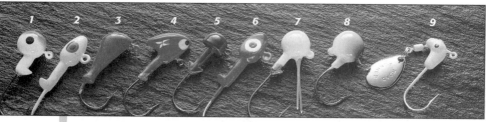

POPULAR HEAD STYLES include: (1) ball, a good all-around choice; (2) bullet, which cuts easily through current; (3) banana, with a sharp kicking action for vertical jigging; (4) stand-up, for snaggy bottoms; (5) mushroom, good for soft-plastic tails; (6) keel, sinks rapidly and easily slices through current; (7) weedless, brushguard protects jig from catching on weeds and brush; (8) stinger-hook jig, short shank jig works well with live-bait and stinger hooks short striking fish; (9) pony or spinnertype, provides extra flash and sound.

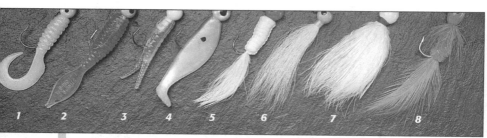

POPULAR DRESSINGS include: (1) curlytail; (2) paddletail grub; (3) split-tail grub; (4) shad; and (5) grub with marabou tail, a good choice for tipping because the tail does not cover the bait. These soft plastics feel like real food so walleyes will hold on longer, giving you more time to set the hook. (6) Bucktail is durable and sinks slowly. (7) Marabou has a unique breathing action. (8) Chenille-and-feather jigs are also good for tipping.

a sharp tap to merely a gradual tightening of the line. An active fish inhales a jig by sucking in water and expelling it through the gills. This type of strike produces the sharp-tap sensation. When a walleye is not actively feeding, it simply swims up and closes its mouth over the jig, causing the line to tighten.

Beginning jig fishermen fail to set the hook on a high percentage of their strikes. They expect to feel a sharp tug, as they would if using a crankbait or spinner. But a walleye usually grabs a jig as it sinks, not as it moves forward. So if you wait for a sharp tug before setting the hook, you will seldom catch a walleye on a jig.

The best policy is to set the hook whenever you feel anything unusual. If you hop the jig off bottom, but it does not sink as you would expect, a walleye has probably grabbed it. What seems like excess drag from a weed may turn out to be a walleye. And a slight peck that feels like a perch bite could be the trophy of a lifetime.

The secret to detecting subtle strikes is to keep your line taut while the jig is sinking. If you twitch your rod tip, then drop it back rapidly as the jig sinks, slack will form and you will not feel the strike. Instead, lower the jig with tension on the line, as if you were setting it gently on bottom.

You will detect more strikes if you carefully watch your line and rod tip. Many times, you will see a strike that you cannot feel. If you see the line twitch where it enters the water, or if the line moves slightly to the side, set the hook.

One of the big problems in jig fishing is noticing strikes on a windy day. The wind forms a belly in your line and buffets your rod tip, so a slight twitch often goes unnoticed. To keep the problem to a minimum, hold your rod tip low. The size of the belly will be much smaller, and the rod tip will not whip around as much.

Selecting the proper rod is vital to successful jig fishing. Most experts prefer a sensitive graphite spinning rod to detect delicate strikes. A rod about 6 feet long with a light tip and stiff butt is a good all-around choice. The light tip responds to a subtle tap, yet the powerful butt enables you to sink the hook with a slight snap of the wrists.

Line is also important. Limp, premium-grade monofilament from 6- to 8-pound test works well in most situations. Stiffer or heavier line comes off your reel in coils, so it is almost impossible to keep your line tight. Many anglers prefer fluorescent mono for jig fishing because it is easy to see. But in clear water, fluorescent line will result in fewer strikes. You can see your line better if you wear polarized glasses.

Attach your line to a jig with some type of clinch knot or with a loop knot. A loop knot lets the jig pivot freely at the attachment eye, maximizing the action. Do not use a heavy snap, a snap swivel or a steel leader. They add weight and are more visible than plain mono.

One of the most common mistakes in jig fishing for walleyes is using a jig that is too heavy. A light jig sinks more slowly, so walleyes have more time to grab it. As a rule, use the lightest jig you can keep on bottom. In most cases, you will need about 1/8 ounce for every 10 feet of depth. You will need a heavier jig to stay on bottom when fishing in wind or current.

HOW TO CAST AND RETRIEVE A JIG FOR WALLEYES

•*Lift* the jig with a slight twitch of the rod tip after letting it sink to bottom. How high you hop the jig depends on the mood of the fish. When they are lethargic, a steady retrieve may work better than a hopping retrieve.

•*Lower* the rod tip, keeping the line taut as the jig sinks. If you do not keep tension on the line, you will not feel the strike. Continue to lift and lower, reeling up a few inches of line after each hop.

•*Strikes* come on the drop. If the fish inhales the jig, you will feel a sharp tap and the rod tip will twitch noticeably.

HOW TO TIP A JIG WITH LIVE BAIT

TIP a jig with a minnow by (1) pushing the hook through the lips, from the bottom up. To keep a minnow on the jig longer, (2) hook it through the eye sockets. The most secure method of attaching a minnow is to (3) push the hook of a plain jig into the mouth and up through the back. Hook a leech (4) through the sucker end. Attach a nightcrawler by (5) hooking it through the tip of the head; (6) hooking it through the middle so that

If the fish hits gently, the line will tighten slightly or the jig will not sink as expected.

•*Set the hook* immediately when you feel anything unusual; a walleye spits a jig quickly. A flick of the wrists results in a faster hook set than a long sweep of the arms, but you will need a stiff rod to sink the hook.

WHEN AND HOW TO USE A STINGER

•*Check* your minnow for teeth marks or ripped skin if you had a strike but failed to hook the fish. Damaged skin on the rear half of the minnow means that walleyes are striking short and that you should tie on a stinger.

•*Make* a stinger by tying a short piece of mono from the bend of the jig's hook to a size 10 treble hook. Hook the minnow as shown above.

both ends trail; or (7) threading it onto a plain jig, pushing the nightcrawler head as far up the shaft as possible. (8) Hook a waterdog through the lips with the jig hook and push a stinger, usually a size 10 treble hook, into the tail. Note: All the baits shown above have been hooked on plain jig heads so the hooking method is clear. But each of these methods except numbers 3 and 7 will also work with any short-tailed jig.

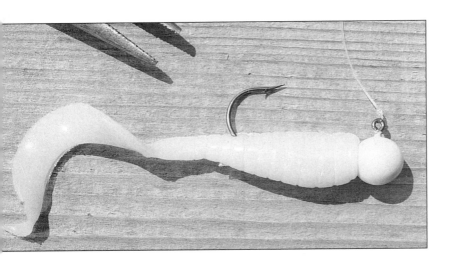

OTHER JIG-FISHING TIPS

•*Store* jig heads and soft plastic tails in small zip-lock bags. The bags are watertight, so the jig hooks will not rust. Tails stored this way will not discolor and can be treated with worm oil so they stay pliable.

•*Bend* the point of the jig hook slightly outward if you are having trouble hooking walleyes (above). The extra clearance between the hook point and the head of the jig will improve your hooking percentage.

Fishing with Jigging Lures

Of all the artificial lures used for walleyes, jigging lures may be the most underrated. Although commonly used on reservoirs and big rivers, these lures are seldom seen on natural lakes.

Unlike most jigs, jigging lures have built-in action. A vibrating blade wiggles rapidly; a tailspin has a spinner blade on the rear that rotates as the lure moves forward and as it sinks; a jigging spoon rocks when pulled upward and tumbles erratically when it settles toward bottom.

These lures usually work best when jigged vertically. Walleyes strike a jigging lure as it sinks, much the same way they strike a jig, so a taut line is crucial if you are to detect a strike. You can also troll or cast with jigging lures. Make long, fast sweeps with your rod tip, then let the lure settle back.

Vibrating blades are often more effective than jigs in murky water. Walleyes detect the wiggle with their lateral-line sense even if they cannot see the lure. Because vibrating blades sink rapidly, they work well in deep water or swift current. These qualities make them perfectly suited to the swift, murky water of most rivers.

Attach a vibrating blade with a plain, round-nosed snap inserted through one of the line-attachment holes on the back. You can change the amount of wiggle by attaching the snap in different holes. The rear hole produces the widest wiggle; the front hole the narrowest.

Tailspins work best in water that is relatively clear. The added flash and vibration of the spinner blade may trigger a walleye that is not interested in a jig. Tie a tailspin directly to your line.

Jigging spoons will take walleyes when jigged vertically in flooded timber. They can also be used for walleyes suspended in open water. Attach a jigging spoon to your line with a split-ring.

You can use the same tackle when fishing with jigging lures as you would when fishing with jigs. But many anglers prefer a slightly longer and stiffer rod, such as a 6 1/2-foot bait-casting rod, and heavier line, usually 8- to 10-pound mono.

> QUICK TIP: Jig vertically with a jigging lure by sweeping it sharply upward, then letting it settle with a taut line. As it settles, watch your line for a twitch, sideways movement or slack. Then set the hook immediately.

Fishing with Plugs

Plugs are a recent addition to the arsenal of many walleye fishermen, but the idea of using plugs to catch walleyes is not exactly new. In fact, past generations of walleye anglers relied almost exclusively on trolling plugs.

As live bait became more widely used, plugs lost popularity. But with the introduction of many new plug types and the improvement of existing types, plugs have regained favor with walleye anglers.

Walleyes normally prefer plugs from 3 to 6 inches long, although big walleyes will take plugs as long as 8 inches. The plugs most commonly used in walleye fishing are minnow plugs, crankbaits, vibrating plugs and trolling plugs.

MINNOW PLUGS. The long, slender shape of these plugs has a special appeal to walleyes because it resembles the shape of perch, ciscoes, shiners and other common walleye foods. And the tight wobble, even at a slow retrieve speed, gives minnow plugs a remarkably lifelike appearance.

Minnow plugs come in the following styles for fishing under various conditions:

•*Short-lipped floating models* run at depths of 5 feet or less. They work best for casting or trolling over shallow shoals and weedbeds.

•*Long-lipped floating models* dive as deep as 20 feet, and are generally used for trolling along deep structure or over deep weedbeds.

•*Sinking models* can be trolled in deep water, or counted down to a specific depth and retrieved at that level.

•*Neutrally buoyant models* can be retrieved very slowly without floating to the surface or sinking. When walleyes are inactive, a neutrally buoyant plug may work better than a floating or sinking type. Because neutrally buoyant plugs can be retrieved so slowly, they catch walleyes at water temperatures down to 40°F. Other types of minnow plugs become effective at about 45°F.

Walleyes seem to favor the action of short-lipped floaters. When fishing in deep water, many anglers attach sinkers ahead of short-lipped floaters instead of using diving or sinking models.

Minnow plugs are light for their size, so they are difficult to cast. But you can improve your casting distance by using light line, usually 6-pound test, and a 6½- to 7½-foot spinning rod with a light tip. The long rod

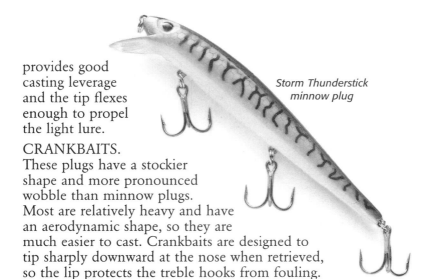

Storm Thunderstick
minnow plug

provides good casting leverage and the tip flexes enough to propel the light lure.

CRANKBAITS. These plugs have a stockier shape and more pronounced wobble than minnow plugs. Most are relatively heavy and have an aerodynamic shape, so they are much easier to cast. Crankbaits are designed to tip sharply downward at the nose when retrieved, so the lip protects the treble hooks from fouling.

Crankbaits come in the same four styles as minnow plugs. Comparable styles of crankbaits and minnow plugs are fished under much the same conditions. Crankbaits, however, generally require a faster retrieve to achieve their intense wobble. As a result, they work best at higher water temperatures, usually above 55°F.

Before attempting to fish with a crankbait, test it to make sure it is properly tuned. If the plug is out of tune, it will not track straight and cannot run at maximum depth. To tune a crankbait, simply bend the attachment eye away from the direction in which the plug veers.

A 6- to 6½-foot spinning outfit with 8- to 10-pound mono is adequate for most crankbait fishing, but a stiff bait-casting rod works better for deep divers that have a strong pull.

VIBRATING PLUGS. The rapid wiggle of these plugs sets up vibrations that attract walleyes even in the murkiest water. Many have internal shot or beads to produce sound.

Most vibrating plugs sink, so you can fish them at virtually any depth. Like crankbaits, they must be retrieved rapidly to attain maximum action, so they are most effective at temperatures above 55°F.

Vibrating plugs have little wind resistance, so they cast easily. Models with internal shot will cast even farther and sink more quickly, so they are a good choice for casting or trolling along deep structure.

Vibrating plugs are normally fished with rods, reels and line similar to those used with crankbaits.

TROLLING PLUGS. Most of these plugs have broad foreheads which produce a wide wobbling action. But the broad forehead also adds wind resistance, making them difficult to cast.

Without added weight, trolling plugs run at depths ranging from 5 to 20 feet. Some are designed for slow trolling, others for speed trolling. Models used for speed trolling work best at temperatures of 70°F or higher.

Medium-powered spinning or baitcasting gear with 8- to 10-pound mono performs well with most trolling plugs. But for speed trolling, you will need a stiff baitcasting rod with low-stretch mono of at least 12-pound test.

For best action, attach all plugs with a split-ring, a round-nosed snap or a loop knot. If you snub your knot directly to the attachment eye, you will dampen the plug's action.

BASIC PLUG-FISHING TECHNIQUES

•*Locate* walleyes by trolling parallel to a breakline. To cover a wide range of depths, one fisherman trolls a deep-diving plug on the outside, another trolls a shallow-running plug on the inside and a third casts a shallow runner over weeds or rocky shoals.

•*Cast* your plug downwind while drifting over a shoal or weedbed or along a breakline. If necessary, use an electric motor to control your drift. Casting with the wind gives you more distance and keeps you from casting into water through which your boat has drifted.

•*Troll* against the wind or current whenever possible. Walleyes generally prefer a slow-moving plug, and trolling this way reduces your speed. If you troll with the wind or current, precise steering will be difficult. And trolling with the current will also cause your plug to lose action.

TIPS FOR FISHING WITH PLUGS

•*Pinch* a split-shot on the front screw-eye after removing

the treble hook. The shot makes the plug cast easier and run deeper. If the shot is the right size, the plug will be neutrally buoyant. Removing the treble also reduces tangling on the cast and snagging on the retrieve.

• *Vary* the action and speed of a plug by periodically sweeping your rod tip forward, then dropping it back. The change often triggers a strike from a walleye that has been following the plug. This technique works equally well for casting or trolling.

During low-light conditions, walleyes often move to shallow rock reefs to feed. Casting plugs over these reefs is the best way to catch these active fish.

Other Artificial Lures

A walleye will, on occasion, strike any type of artificial lure. Muskie fishermen sometimes hook trophy-class walleyes while pitching foot-long jerkbaits. Bass anglers often catch walleyes while fishing along weedlines with plastic worms. Bluegill fishermen have even taken walleyes on tiny wet flies.

Although jigs, jigging lures and plugs are the most widely used artificials, others like spinners and flies may be equally effective.

Weight-forward spinners (page 109) can be used at a variety of depths. They are well-suited to unstratified waters, where walleyes may range from 5 to 30 feet deep. Most weight-forward spinners come with a plain hook for use with nightcrawlers or other live bait, but some have tail dressings of hair, feathers or soft plastic, making bait unnecessary. The best sizes for walleyes are 1/4 to 5/8 ounce.

Standard in-line spinners work well in spring, when walleyes are in the shallows. Models with size 2 or 3 blades are most effective.

Spinnerbaits are more snag-resistant than other types of spinners. Models weighing 1/8 to 1/4 ounce will catch walleyes that are buried in weeds or brush.

Streamer flies produce walleyes in spring. They imitate baitfish, so a walleye cruising the shallows in search of food finds a streamer hard to resist.

HOW TO USE OTHER ARTIFICIAL LURES

•*Toss* a spinnerbait into pockets in flooded brush or emergent weeds and let it helicopter downward before starting your retrieve. This method works best in rivers and reservoirs, where rising springtime water levels drive walleyes into shoreline vegetation.

•*Cast* a standard in-line spinner into the shallows when walleyes are cruising rocky or gravelly shorelines in early spring (above). Reel just fast enough to keep the lure above bottom. To avoid severe line twist, always attach a standard spinner with a snap swivel.

•*Cast* a streamer over a shallow feeding shoal beginning at dusk. Retrieve with a darting motion. Use a sink-tip fly line, a tapered leader with an 8- to 10-pound tippet, and a size 2 or 4 fly that resembles a baitfish, such as a white marabou muddler.

4

TECHNIQUES FOR
SPECIAL
SITUATIONS

Walleyes in the Weeds

In years past, few walleye anglers ever considered fishing in the weeds. They were told at an early age that walleyes always preferred a hard, clean bottom, so that is where they fished. But largemouth bass fishermen knew differently because they often pulled walleyes from the weeds using spinnerbaits, crankbaits and plastic worms.

Even today, the average walleye angler seldom fishes in the weeds. Many do not realize that walleyes spend a significant amount of time in the weeds; others think that walleyes in the weeds cannot be caught.

Walleyes move into weeds to find food, shade or cooler temperatures. Many types of baitfish use the weeds for cover, so a walleye cruising through the tangle can easily grab a meal. On a bright day, walleyes can often find adequate shade and cool temperatures in a weedbed, instead of retreating to deep water. The temperature in the weeds may be five degrees cooler than elsewhere in the shallows.

If walleyes are raised in rearing ponds during their first summer of life, they become accustomed to living in weeds. It is possible that these walleyes, after being stocked into a lake, have a greater tendency to live in the weeds than walleyes reared naturally in the lake. If a lake also has natural reproduction, there may be separate populations of weed-dwelling and reef-dwelling walleyes.

Weeds produce oxygen, but it is unlikely that walleyes would move into weeds for that reason. Only in rare cases would oxygen levels in shallow water reach levels low enough to affect walleyes, even in waters where there are no weeds.

Eutrophic lakes are most likely to have populations of weed walleyes. Because the depths lose oxygen during the summer, walleyes may have no choice but to remain in the epilimnion where weeds offer the only shade. But you may find weed walleyes in mesotrophic and even in oligotrophic lakes. And walleyes in big rivers frequently feed in weedy backwaters, or in weedbeds in slack pools or along current margins. Occasionally, you will find reservoir walleyes in weeds, but fluctuating water levels prevent most types of weeds from taking root.

Not all weeds attract walleyes. The best weedbeds are in or near deep water. Seldom will you find the fish on a shallow, weedy flat with no deep water nearby. Broadleaf weeds generally hold more walleyes than narrowleaf varieties; submergent weeds more than emergent or floating-leaved types.

You can find walleyes in weeds almost any time of year. But weed fishing is usually best in summer and fall, the times when young-of-the-year baitfish are seeking cover from predators.

TYPES OF WEEDS THAT HOLD WALLEYES

•*Largeleaf pondweed*, sometimes called broadleaf cabbage, grows in water as deep as 14 feet. The leaves are up to 7 inches long and 1½ inches wide. The flowering heads may extend above the surface.

•*Richardson's pondweed*, often called curlyleaf cabbage, grows in water as deep as 10 feet. The wavy leaves are up to 5 inches long and 3/4 inch wide. The flowering heads always extend above the surface.

•*Coontail* grows in water as deep as 30 feet. The plants are not rooted, but grow in large masses on the bottom. Tiny leaves grow in whorls around the stem and are usually forked. There is no flowering head.

•*Water milfoil* grows in water as deep as 30 feet. The plants are usually rooted. Tiny leaves grow in whorls around the stem and are shaped like the veins of a feather. The top of the plant may have small flowers.

•*Chara*, also called sandgrass, or muskgrass because of its skunk-like odor, blankets the bottom in water as deep as 35 feet. Coarse branchlets grow in whorls around the stem and are usually coated with calcium deposits.

•*Hardstem bulrush* grows in water as deep as 5 feet and may extend up to 6 feet above the surface. Dark green in color, the tough-stemmed plants grow only on a firm bottom, usually sand or gravel.

Techniques for Weed Walleyes

Fishing along the edge of the weeds is easy. Simply cast or troll a slip-sinker rig or a jig along the weedline, keeping it as close to the weeds as possible. But when walleyes are actually in the weeds or suspended above them, fishing is much more difficult.

What seems like a bite often turns out to be a weed. If you hook a strand of sandgrass, for instance, tiny branchlets break off as your hook slides along the stem, creating a jerking sensation. On the other hand, what feels like a weed may be a walleye.

If you attempt to fish with live bait, the bait will often come off the hook when you pull free of a weed. And regardless of what technique you use, you will continually have to remove bits of weed from your hook.

Different types of weeds demand different fishing techniques. You can retrieve a lure through some types of weeds without fouling, but other types will catch on the hooks. To fish effectively in weeds, you should be aware of these differences.

HOW WEEDS DIFFER

•*Broadleaf weeds*, including most varieties of cabbage, are crispy enough that a sharp tug will rip the leaf and free your hook.

•*Long, stringy weeds*, such as coontail, are almost impossible to free from your hook. Use a weedless hook or fish only the edges.

•*Brittle narrowleaf weeds* like sandgrass cling to your hook. But a sharp tug will bend the branchlets enough so you can pull free.

HOW TO FISH JIGS IN WEEDS

•*Rip* your jig through tall broadleaf weeds by making a sharp sweep with your rod tip when you feel resistance (below). Any type of jig weighing from $1/16$ to $1/8$ ounce will work, but many anglers prefer pyramid jigs because weeds slide over the head instead of catching on the eye. If the weeds are dense, keep the jig riding above them rather than trying to rip through them.

•*Work* the edges of a bed of long, stringy weeds. These weeds grow in clumps and walleyes often hold in the open water nearby. A jig fished in the weeds would foul continuously.

HOW TO FISH SPINNERS IN THE WEEDS

•*Bait* a mono-leader type spinner with a minnow, leech or nightcrawler. Troll at a slow speed, keeping the rig just above the weedtops. If you feel the rig touching weeds, lift your rod tip. A floating spinner will keep the bait riding higher.

•*Retrieve* a spinnerbait through dense weeds, letting it helicopter to bottom when it comes to a deeper pocket. Use a standard spinnerbait with a minnow or plastic curlytail in place of the skirt, or a safety-pin spinner arm attached to a hair or feather jig.

HOW TO FISH A SLIP-BOBBER IN WEEDS

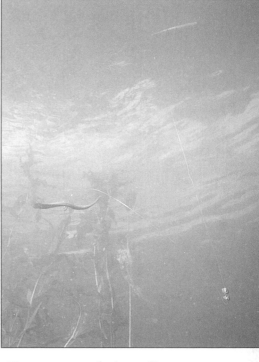

•*Cast* a slip-bobber rig into a pocket in tall broadleaf weeds. Adjust the bobber stop so the bait dangles just above bottom. Slip-bobbers also work well for fishing above a blanket of sandgrass or alongside beds of coontail, milfoil or other long, stringy weeds.

HOW TO FISH OTHER LURES IN THE WEEDS

•*Cast* a shallow-running crankbait or minnow plug over a weedy flat or point, keeping the plug just above the weedtops. Trolling may spook the walleyes. A deep-running crankbait or minnow plug works well for trolling along a deep weedline. Clip the leading hooks to reduce fouling.

•*Tie* a sliding cone-sinker rig, then attach a float ahead of your bait, or hook your bait to a floating jig head. Troll or retrieve over sandgrass or other low-growing weeds. The tapered sinker slips through the weeds and the float or jig head rides above them.

Walleyes in Timber & Brush

In many rivers and reservoirs, timber and brush provide the only shallow-water cover. Weeds are scarce or non-existent, so walleyes rely on timber and brush to provide a supply of food and a shady resting spot.

You can find some walleyes around almost any kind of submerged timber, including flooded trees, stumps, logs on the bottom, and trees toppled into the water from an eroded bank. But your chances of finding good numbers of walleyes will be better if you know what type of timber to look for.

The best timber is near deep water. A timbered flat along the edge of a creek channel, for instance, will hold more walleyes than a timbered flat with no deep water nearby. A

tree toppled into deep water off a steep riverbank will attract more walleyes than a tree toppled onto a shallow sandbar.

Timber may hold walleyes anytime from the prespawn period until late fall. But brush holds walleyes mainly in spring, when high water floods willows and bushes along the bank.

Walleyes move into the brush when the water level begins to rise. As long as the water continues to rise or stabilizes, they remain in the brush. But when the water begins to drop even the slightest bit, they move to deeper water. This movement may be an instinctive reaction, to avoid being trapped in an isolated pool.

Anglers who specialize in fishing timber and brush prefer cone-sinker rigs with weedless hooks, brushguard jigs, or jigs with fine-wire hooks. Other good lures and rigs include spinnerbaits, jigging spoons, slip-bobber rigs, and crankbaits and minnow plugs with clipped trebles.

If you are afraid to drop your bait or lure into the thickest tangle of sticks and logs, you will catch only the most aggressive walleyes, which are also the smallest ones. The bigger walleyes usually hang out where the cover is densest, so you will have to risk losing a few rigs to catch them.

TYPES OF TIMBER AND BRUSH THAT HOLD WALLEYES

•*Toppled trees* with the small branches intact are better than old trees with only large limbs remaining. Walleyes can find baitfish and insects among the small branches.

•*Standing timber* near deep water can hold walleyes, if the trees are close enough together to provide ample shade. Avoid fishing a flat where the trees are widely scattered.

•*Flooded brush* often holds walleyes in high water. The brush itself may be too dense to fish effectively, but you can cast into pockets or work the edges.

TECHNIQUES FOR FISHING IN TIMBER AND BRUSH

•*Rig* a nightcrawler or minnow on a size 4 weedless hook attached to a sliding cone-sinker rig. Then crawl the bait slowly through dense timber or brush. The weedguard will prevent the hook from snagging, and the cone sinker will easily slide through obstructions.

•*Retrieve* a brushguard jig tipped with a pork trailer through toppled trees or standing timber. The jig will seldom hang up, and the trailer will stay on the hook indefinitely. A brushguard prevents snagging in the dense cover but may cause you to miss a few strikes.

•*Cast* a 1/16- to 1/8-ounce jig with a fine-wire hook into a pocket in flooded brush. Tip the jig with a minnow and retrieve slowly, raising your rod tip to avoid snags. A fine-wire hook will improve your hooking percentage, and if it does snag, it will usually bend enough to pull free.

Walleyes on a Rocky Bottom

A bottom of jagged and broken rocks is one of the best places to find walleyes. But it is one of the most difficult places to fish, especially when using live-bait rigs.

With an ordinary slip-sinker rig, the rocks seem to reach out and grab the sinker. You can reduce the frustration and catch a lot more walleyes by using the following techniques:

• *Suspend* your bait from a slip-bobber. Position your bobber stop so the bait hangs just above the rocks.

• *When trolling*, lower your rig to the bottom, then reel in a foot or two so the sinker does not drag on the rocks. Occasionally drop your rod tip back until the sinker touches the rocks, to make sure the depth has not changed.

• *Float* your bait off bottom with a floating jig head or some other type of floating rig, or use an inflated nightcrawler. For extra flotation, hook the crawler through the middle and inject both ends with air. A floating rig will keep your hook out of the rocks but will not prevent your sinker from snagging.

SMALL JIGS are effective in the rocks, if you do not let them drag bottom. Keep the jig swimming just above the rocks; let it touch occasionally to check the depth. If you use a heavy jig, it will quickly wedge in the rocks. You may lose a few small jigs, but they are less expensive than most other lures.

SNAG-RESISTANT SINKERS include: (1) Bait Walker™, (2) bottom bouncer, (3) Flex-O-Drop sinker, (4) pencil lead on 3-way swivel rig, (5) dropper with split-shot.

•*Use* a snag-resistant sinker (above), or use a Wolf River rig (page 113) tied with a dropper lighter than the standing line. When you get snagged, you lose only the sinker instead of the entire rig.

•*Use* tough, abrasion-resistant monofilament instead of soft, limp mono. Soft line nicks too easily when fished over rocks.

Some types of artificial lures also work well over rocky bottoms. Small jigs, floating crankbaits and weight-forward spinners are among the best choices. Select a crankbait that will run just above the rocks. If the lure should hit a rock, the lip will usually keep it from snagging. With a weight-forward spinner, reel just fast enough to keep it off bottom. By tipping it with a nightcrawler, you can increase its buoyancy and fish it more slowly.

QUICK TIP: Substitute a mono dropper (#5 in above photo) for a slip-sinker. Tie a barrel swivel on one end of the dropper and pinch split-shot on the other. If the split-shot snag, give a strong tug to slide them off the dropper, then pinch on new ones.

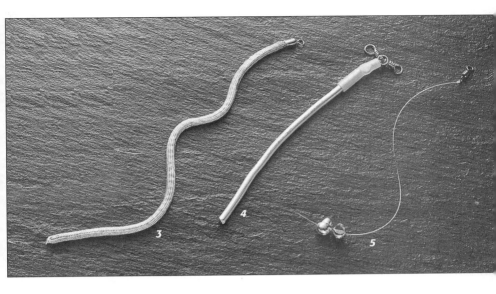

HOW LINE ANGLE AFFECTS SNAGGING

•*Keep* your line as close to vertical as possible when fishing on a rocky bottom. When trolling with a light sinker, you must let out a lot of line to reach bottom. Because your line is at a low angle, your sinker can easily wedge between the rocks (below, left). With a heavier sinker, you can use a much shorter line. The line is at a greater angle to the bottom, so the sinker usually climbs over the rocks instead of wedging between them (below, right).

143

Suspended Walleyes

For generations, the basic rule of walleye fishing was keep your bait on the bottom. But modern-day walleye anglers know that this is not always good advice. Walleyes may suspend off bottom for any of the following reasons:

TEMPERATURE. In a clear lake, walleyes retreat to deeper water after feeding to avoid sunlight. But in low- to moderate-clarity water, they often move laterally rather than vertically, especially if the water is stratified into temperature layers. By moving laterally, they can avoid drastic temperature changes.

Walleyes that feed on reefs, for instance, often suspend in nearby open water when feeding is completed. They usually move less than 100 yards. Many fishermen make the mistake of assuming that the walleyes have moved deeper, so they waste a great deal of time searching barren water.

OXYGEN. If the deep water lacks sufficient oxygen in summer, and there is a shortage of shallow-water structure, walleyes may have no choice but to suspend.

TOXIC GASES. Walleyes often suspend on calm, sunny days in summer. Many anglers have witnessed this behavior and wondered about the cause.

In many instances, the fish are suspending to avoid high levels of toxic gases near bottom. Calm, sunny weather allows maximum sunlight penetration. Sunlight promotes decomposition of organic bottom sediments, which produces levels of carbon dioxide, hydrogen sulfide and methane gas that could be toxic to walleyes.

To escape, walleyes suspend above the layer of toxic gases. If the bottom is rich in organic materials, they may move up as much as 10 feet.

HOW A DEPTH FINDER CAN HELP YOU FIND SUSPENDED WALLEYES

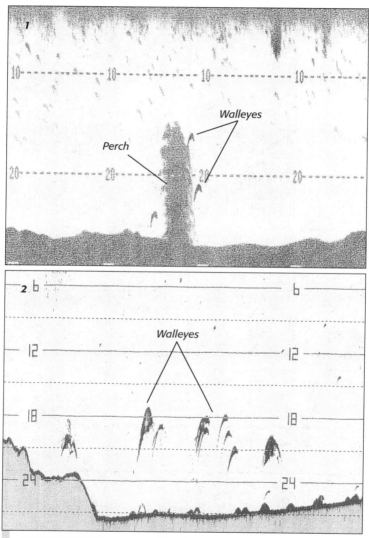

DEPTH FINDERS can provide clues to how walleyes suspend. Frame 1 shows plumes of small yellow perch, a favorite walleye food, reaching from the bottom almost to the surface. You can see walleyes suspended at various depths alongside the perch. Frame 2 shows walleyes that have moved laterally into open water in order to stay in the same temperature zone where they fed earlier in the day.

In windy weather, water circulation prevents toxic gases from accumulating, so walleyes need not suspend to avoid the gases.

FOOD. The walleye's favorite foods are not necessarily linked to the bottom. Open-water baitfish like shad and ciscoes, for example, can be found at almost any depth. On calm mornings or evenings, you may see baitfish schools dimpling the surface. Walleyes will ignore their oxygen and temperature preferences for an easy meal, so they pursue the baitfish in open water or hang just below the surface schools. Walleyes may suspend to feed on immature insects, particularly emerging mayfly nymphs.

How to Catch Suspended Walleyes

Finding and catching suspended walleyes can be a difficult assignment. Walleyes suspended off structure are there to rest, not to feed. Walleyes suspended in pursuit of baitfish are willing to bite, but they may not notice your bait among the clouds of natural food.

To catch suspended walleyes, you must present the right bait or lure at precisely the right depth. Finding this depth requires either a graph or flasher or a lot of experimentation.

One of the simplest ways to catch suspended walleyes is to use a slip-bobber rig. Set your bobber stop at the appropriate depth, bait up with a leech, nightcrawler or minnow, and wait for a bite. This technique works especially well for walleyes that are not actively feeding.

If the walleyes are within a few feet of bottom, you can float your bait up to them rather than lowering it down. Most anglers use a slip-sinker rig with some type of floating jig head or a float that attaches to the leader.

The major drawback to these floating rigs is the difficulty of controlling the depth. In most cases, the bait will not float nearly as high as you would expect. To get an idea of how high it will float, try trolling alongside the boat in shallow, clear water. You can make the bait float higher by increasing the amount of flotation, lengthening the leader or reducing the boat speed.

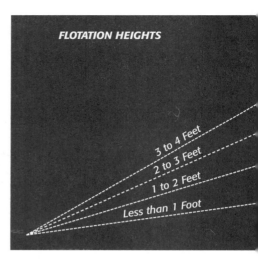

FLOTATION HEIGHTS

3 to 4 Feet
2 to 3 Feet
1 to 2 Feet
Less than 1 Foot

You can also catch walleyes that are within a few feet of bottom by jigging vertically with a vibrating blade or tailspin. While drifting with the wind, jig with long sweeps of the rod; keep the line taut as the lure sinks to bottom.

You can catch walleyes suspended at any depth by casting or trolling with vibrating plugs, jigs, vibrating blades and weight-forward spinners. To locate walleyes with these lures, use the countdown technique. Many fishermen prefer to tip their jigs and spinners with live bait.

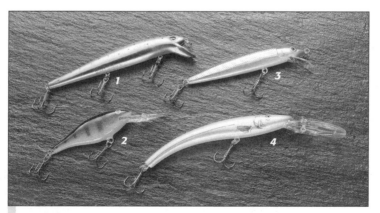

POPULAR PLUGS for suspended walleyes include models that run less than 5 feet deep such as a (1) Thunderstick™. Models that run from 6 to 10 feet include a (2) Shad Rap™. Suspending lures, such as a (3) Husky Jerk™, are retrieved to the desired depth and then will remain at that depth when stopped. Models that run deeper than 10 feet include a (4) Reef Runner™.

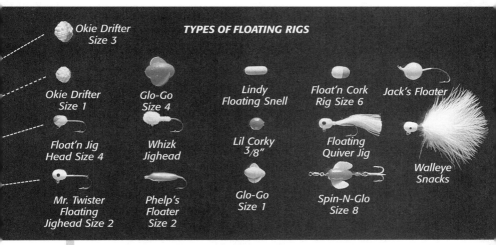

TYPES OF FLOATING RIGS

Okie Drifter
Size 3

Okie Drifter
Size 1

Glo-Go
Size 4

Lindy
Floating Snell

Float'n Cork
Rig Size 6

Jack's Floater

Float'n Jig
Head Size 4

Whizk
Jighead

Lil Corky
3/8"

Floating
Quiver Jig

Walleye
Snacks

Mr. Twister
Floating
Jighead Size 2

Phelp's
Floater
Size 2

Glo-Go
Size 1

Spin-N-Glo
Size 8

FLOTATION of various floating rigs was determined in tests by the research staff for this book. Each rig was tied to a 10-foot leader of 8-pound monofilament, baited with a medium-sized leech, then trolled at a slow speed (1.5 feet per second). The long leader was used to accentuate differences in flotation. With a shorter leader, the heights would be reduced in proportion to leader length. The same rigs baited with minnows and nightcrawlers yielded similar results. The height that each rig floated above bottom is shown in the above chart.

TIPS ON FISHING FOR SUSPENDED WALLEYES

•*Thread* half of a nightcrawler onto the hook of a weight-forward spinner. To prevent short strikes, the worm should trail no more than an inch behind the hook.

•*Inject* air just below the collar of a nightcrawler to make it float. If you inject air into the tail or over-inflate the worm, it will look unnatural. Use a worm blower or hypodermic needle.

•*Yo-yo* a split-shot rig baited with a leech or nightcrawler through a school of suspended walleyes. Use as little weight as possible so the bait does not sink too fast.

Planer Boards

Lifelong jig fishermen cringe at the thought of connecting their line to a board and dragging crankbaits around the lake with their outboards attempting to trigger walleyes into striking. But for anglers wanting to catch fish on days and in places that wouldn't produce very many walleyes using other techniques, learning how to fish with planer boards is a good idea.

Planer boards allow anglers to expand their coverage area at multiple depths. They not only work well to reach walleyes in clearwater areas where fish are spooky or on large flats, but also work very well to catch walleyes suspended in open water.

IN-LINE BOARDS. The angler's line is attached to a clothespinlike clip on the board, sending the line off to the side of the boat. This enables the angler to cover a wider area and run lures through water undisturbed by the boat.

By design, the boards either angle left or right when trolled. They attach to the line by a release clip, a pinch or twist clip that attaches to 10- to 12-pound line without damaging it, even when a fish strikes. Most walleye anglers prefer to attach the clip tight to the line so it doesn't release when a fish strikes. If a board does release, anglers will have to go back to retrieve it, often in waves or at night. Some manufacturers make lights that easily attach to the flag portion of the boards so they can easily be found at night.

Mono, lead core and superlines are the most popular lines when using planer boards. Because of their thin diameter, superlines often pull free from most board release clips when fish strike. Wrap the line twice around the clip to keep the board attached to the line, eliminating the need to relocate the board at night or in waves. A bouncing, bobbing or dipping board usually means there is a fish on. To land the fish, slowly reel in the line until the board

151

TIPS FOR USING PLANERS

USE a snap-swivel at the back end of an in-line board to con-
nect to the line. When a fish trips the release, the board will
slide down the line as you reel in the fish.

ATTACH multiple lines to a ski-type board using sliding release
clips (inset). Often these larger planer boards are run off a
mast on the boat.

reaches the boat. Detach the board, and continue fighting and landing the fish. While planer boards are most often used to catch walleyes on large flats, they are equally effective on suspended fish. When trolling with side planers, a turn in either direction causes the inside or outside lures to run at different depths and speeds, which often triggers fish. With sinkers attached to the lines, lures and live bait rigs can be run off of planer boards to reach fish suspending 40 to 50 feet beneath the surface.

Anglers also use planers to run their baits into shallow areas where fish would normally spook from boat traffic. Slowly trolling live bait shallow 15 to 20 yards behind the planer board is a good method to catch walleyes in 2 to 5 feet of water.

SKI-TYPE BOARDS. Big double and triple ski-type boards are towed on 200-pound-test lines attached to a mast and reel system at the bow of the boat. These big boards are generally run out on either side and are set out to a desired distance behind the boat. The line is then pinched on a release clip that hangs on the tow line running to the board from the mast. Once the line is set in the jaws of the clip, the ring is hooked over the tow line and the lure pulls the ring down the tow line, taking it and fishing line out until the reel is engaged. Multiple lines can be set in the same manner on the same tow line to cover even a larger area of water in the same pass. Big ski-type boards aren't used by walleye anglers as much as are the smaller in-line type boards. However, the larger boards work well for pulling heavy lead core and for trolling multiple lines.

Effectively being able to cover lots of water with planer boards takes practice and experience. The same will apply to properly trolling boards without tangling and crossing lines. When beginning to learn, never make sharp turns. Long, gradual turns will prevent multiple lines from crossing and tangling. Anglers who acquire the skills of using planer boards broaden their walleye-catching skills to another dimension and will be able to catch more fish in a variety of situations.

Downriggers & Diving Planers

I n deep clearwater lakes, anglers often use downriggers or diving planers to reach walleyes that are roaming the depths in search of food. This specialized equipment is not only easy to use but very effective for precisely presenting spoons, crankbaits and spinners to a desired depth.

DOWNRIGGERS. Downriggers range from portable clamp-on units to electronic retrieval systems capable of raising and lowering the weights, called downrigger balls, by the push of a button. There are also those that "jig" the lure up and down to add to the lure action, and bottom-tracking systems with auto depth setting, to maintain a consistent distance off of the bottom. These electric or winch-style winding systems hold the wire cable that lowers the downrigger balls, which usually weigh 2 to 10 pounds, down to depths in excess of 100 feet.

To use a downrigger, simply let out the lure 40 to 60 feet behind the moving boat, insert the monofilament fishing line into a clip-release mechanism, and lower the ball while at the same time letting out the line from the reel.

When the desired depth is reached, secure the downrigger ball, engage the reel and put the rod in the rod holder. Finally, reel in enough of the line so there is a substantial bend in the rod, but not so much that it causes the line to release from the clip.

When a fish strikes, the line will release from the clip and the loaded rod will assist with the hook set. The best rods for this purpose are durable and have light or medium actions.

Release clips come in two basic types: those that attach directly to the cannonball and those that fasten to the downrigger cable. The latter, which are often called stacker releases, come with two clips that allow anglers to set multiple lines on a cable: one clip attaching to the wire cable and the other to the fishing line.

While most release clips have tension adjustments, walleyes often do not strike the line hard enough to release the line from the clip. To solve this problem, many anglers use a #12 rubber band between their line and the release clip (photo on opposite page). Walleyes should be able to easily break the rubber band to indicate strikes.

Whenever possible, walleye anglers should use 10- to 12-pound mono, which won't be damaged when a fish releases it from the jaws of the clip.

Downriggers enable anglers to target schools of suspended walleyes that rarely see fishing lures. These unpressured, aggressive fish are often some of the biggest the lake or reservoir has to offer.

DIVING PLANERS. Another consistent way to send a lure to a desired depth is to use a diving planer, which attaches fairly close to the lure (5 to 10 feet) and can send it down to a maximum depth of 60 feet.

Some diving planers, like the Dipsy Diver, plane down and off to the side of the boat. Twisting an adjustable dial on the planer causes it to change the diving angle from left or right. The more it is set to run to the side, the shallower it runs. A trip mechanism with an adjustable tension setting releases when a fish strikes to free the tension of the disc against the water, allowing anglers to fight the fish directly.

Diving planers have considerable water resistance and must be fished on heavy line and tackle. Most anglers prefer monofilament lines with breaking strengths from 14 to 30 pounds and 7- to 8-foot soft-action salmon-type rods, which are generally set in rod holders because of the enormous amount of drag caused by the pulling planer.

Spoons, spinners and shallow-running crankbaits run well with diving planers. Lures that won't cause the planer to run other than the way it was designed are the best choice. Deep-diving crankbaits often pull on the planer, causing it to run in an undesirable manner.

Compared to downriggers, diving planers are less precise in their ability to take lures to a particular depth. However, diving planers are inexpensive and therefore the number-one choice of many anglers faced with deepwater walleyes.

TIPS FOR USING DOWNRIGGERS

•*Insert* the line into the release clip, which is lowered down with the ball. Use stacker releases to set multiple lines on one cable.

•*Use* a # 12 rubber band (right) to attach line to releases so smaller fish will release the line. Loop the rubber band around the line and pull tight, then set the loop in the release.

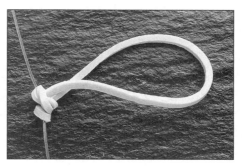

River Fishing

A glance through a list of state-record walleyes reveals that a large number were caught in rivers. There is no doubt that rivers offer some excellent walleye-fishing opportunities. One reason that rivers support good walleye populations is that they generally are not fished as heavily as nearby lakes.

Versatile walleye anglers spend their time fishing in rivers when cold fronts have slowed the action in their favorite lakes. Cold fronts do not seem to have as much effect on river walleyes. Rivers are also a good bet in late summer, when lake fishing may be poor due to high water temperatures and hefty crops of forage fish. When lake walleyes are

scattered because of the fall turnover, river walleyes continue to feed in the same places where you found them in summer.

In the North, portions of many big rivers stay open through the winter months. Walleyes congregate in the tailwaters of dams and around warmwater discharges all winter long, offering the only open-water fishing opportunity.

Inexperienced anglers have more trouble learning to fish in rivers than in lakes. Many do poorly on their first trip to a river, so they do not come back. The secret to catching river walleyes is knowing how current and fluctuating water levels affect their behavior, and adjusting your tactics accordingly.

CURRENT. Walleyes will tolerate a slight current, but seldom will you find them in fast water, unless there is some type of cover to serve as a current break. When searching for walleyes in rivers, you can immediately eliminate a good share of the water because the current is too swift. Just how much current walleyes will tolerate depends on the season.

You can find river walleyes in slack pools, in eddies or downstream from some type of current break like an island, a bridge pier or a large boulder. But many anglers make the mistake of fishing only the downstream side of obstructions. For instance, walleyes usually hold just upstream of a wingdam, a rocky structure intended to deflect current toward the middle of the river to keep the channel from silting in. Current deflecting off the face of a wingdam or other current break creates a slack pocket on the upstream side, providing an ideal spot for a walleye to grab drifting food.

Current edges are to a river what structure is to a lake. Walleyes will hold along the margin between slack and moving water. This way, they can rest in the still water and occasionally dart into the current to get a meal.

FLUCTUATING WATER LEVELS. Most good river fishermen prefer low, stable water for walleye fishing. Under these conditions, the water is at its clearest, and the walleyes are concentrated in well-known spots.

A rapidly changing water level caused by a heavy rain or release of water through a dam can turn a productive walleye hole into dead water. The increase in flow changes the current patterns and drives the walleyes to different areas.

But if you know where to find walleyes when the water is rising, fishing can actually be better than when the water is stable. Rising water often triggers a feeding spree because of the worms, insects and other foods that are washed into the river.

Rising water also causes walleyes to move shallower. They often feed near the base of flooded willows or brush, sometimes in water only a foot deep. If current in the main channel becomes too swift, the fish move into backwater lakes, oxbows, sloughs or cuts where there is practically no current. Or they may swim into the mouths of feeder creeks that are normally dry.

If the increase in flow causes the river to become extremely muddy, walleyes cannot see well enough to find your bait. In many cases, the muddy water comes from a tributary stream. You may be able to find clearer water by moving upstream of the tributary or far enough downstream so the mud has a chance to settle out.

WHERE TO FIND WALLEYES AT DIFFERENT WATER STAGES

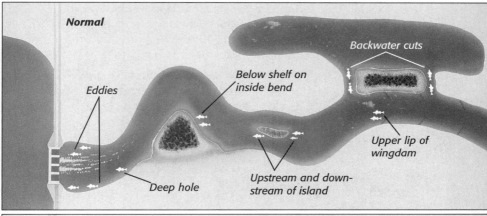

Normal

Eddies

Below shelf on inside bend

Backwater cuts

Upper lip of wingdam

Deep hole

Upstream and down-stream of island

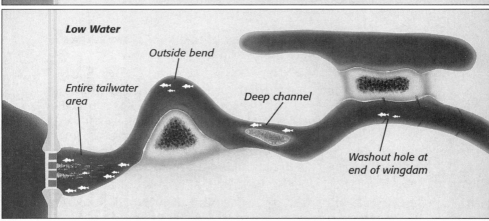

Low Water

Outside bend

Entire tailwater area

Deep channel

Washout hole at end of wingdam

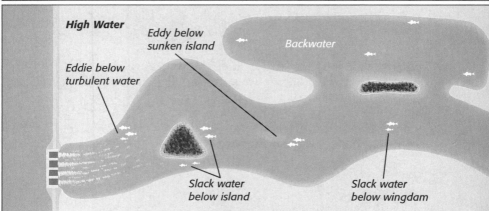

High Water

Eddy below sunken island

Backwater

Eddie below turbulent water

Slack water below island

Slack water below wingdam

Walleyes continue to feed as long as the water level is rising or stable. But when it begins to fall, they immediately sense the change and move to deeper water to avoid getting trapped in a dead-water pool. Once they move deeper, feeding slows and fishing becomes much tougher.

River walleyes are predictable in that they generally move to the same areas at a given water stage. By keeping a log book, you can look back to see where you found fish at a similar stage in previous years. Most sizable rivers have water-level gauges that will give you an exact reading.

Techniques for River Walleyes

With a few modifications, many of the popular techniques for catching walleyes in lakes will also work in rivers.

JIG FISHING. More river walleyes are taken on jigs than on any other lure, but the best sizes and styles may differ from those used to catch walleyes in lakes. In still water, you can easily reach bottom in 15 feet of water with a 1/8-ounce jig, but you will need a 1/4-ounce jig to reach the same depth in moderate current. Most anglers prefer round-head or bullet-head jigs for fishing in current because these types have less water resistance than others.

Jigs are normally fished by casting from an anchored position just upstream of a pool or eddy, by casting to pools and eddies while slipping downstream, by vertically jigging while drifting with the current or by jig trolling.

When jig trolling, motor downstream slightly faster than the current while hopping the jig along bottom. Although most types of lures work best trolled upstream, jigs are more effective trolled downstream. Because you can keep your line closer to vertical, you can hop the jig farther off bottom and detect strikes much easier. When casting a jig from an anchored boat, an upstream retrieve is best. Retrieved downstream, the jig would drag along bottom and quickly snag.

A jig tipped with a minnow usually works well in spring, when the water temperature is below 45°F. But at warmer temperatures, an untipped jig often works better, especially if the water is on the murky side. Under these conditions, walleyes strike at any kind of movement, and tipping with live bait only

QUICK TIP: Retrieve a jig upstream. This way, it sinks slowly, giving the fish time to strike.

reduces your hooking percentage. Fluorescent colors seem to be a bigger attraction than live bait.

FISHING WITH VIBRATING BLADES. Vibrating blades are well-suited to river fishing because they sink rapidly in the current and emit vibrations which attract walleyes even if the water is muddy. They work best when jigged vertically while drifting with the current. But they can also be fished by anchoring upstream of a pool or eddy, casting downstream, then jigging against the current as you would with a lead-head jig.

PLUG FISHING. Trolling with crankbaits, minnow plugs and vibrating plugs accounts for a tremendous number of river walleyes. If the current is not too swift, you can often catch fish by trolling along the edges of the main channel. Other productive trolling areas include long riprap banks, edges of long sandbars and islands, and rocky shorelines.

When trolling with plugs, always move against the current. Much has been written about the logic of trolling with the current because fish are accustomed to seeing their food drifting at them. But experienced river fishermen know that a plug trolled with the current will seldom catch a walleye. Trolling against the current gives the plug good action and enables you to move much more slowly.

Because the current is lightest near the bottom, river walleyes seldom suspend. As a result, keeping your plug near the bottom is especially critical in river fishing. Many anglers use lead-core line or heavy sinkers to keep their plugs ticking bottom.

Another productive plug-fishing technique is casting to a riprap or rocky shoreline while the boat drifts with the current. River walleyes often lie tight to the bank, especially if the water is rising. Casting a plug or spinner within a few inches of shore and retrieving rapidly is one of the best techniques for catching these bank-hugging fish.

FISHING WITH LIVE BAIT. If the bottom is relatively clean, you can lower a slip-sinker rig to bottom and drift with the current. Let out just enough line to reach bottom. If you allow your line to drag on bottom, it will be more difficult to detect a bite and you will get snagged more often. If the bottom is strewn with logs, brush and rocks, you will probably do better with a floating rig or some other rig intended for a rocky bottom.

You can also fish a live-bait rig by casting to pools or eddies from an anchored position or while slipping downstream. Many anglers prefer a plain split-shot rig for this type of fishing.

Current

Almost all rivers have murky water at least part of the time. In discolored water, a fluorescent spinner ahead of your bait can make a big difference.

HOW TO FISH IMPORTANT RIVER FEATURES

•*Wingdams* (left) at normal stage should be worked by anchoring as shown, then casting a jig or plug to the upper lip. Walleyes hold just above the wingdam. At low water, work the washout hole at the end of the wingdam. At high water, fish downstream of the wingdam.

•*Small eddies* created by obstructions like points, islands, submerged sandbars and bridge piers are usually fished by anchoring alongside the eddy. Position your boat so you can cast a jig or live-bait rig into the upstream portion of the eddy, then walk it downstream.

•*Large eddies* hold the most walleyes near the slack-water zone, especially in cold-water periods. Upstream is reverse current; downstream, the current resumes its normal flow. Anchor in the slack water, then work the area with a jig.

•*Pools* (below) can be fished by anchoring well upstream, then casting a jig or live-bait rig and retrieving over the upstream lip. Active walleyes lie at the head of the pool to grab drifting food. Let out more anchor line to reach the less active walleyes in the middle of the pool.

Current

•*Fallen trees* and log jams must be worked by anchoring below them, if you cannot reach the eddy from upstream. Because you must retrieve downstream, use a brushguard jig or a jig with a light-wire hook so that you can easily free it from the branches.

•*Warmwater discharges* from power plants and waste-disposal plants attract walleyes during cold-water periods. Using a jig, crankbait or live-bait rig, fish at different distances from the discharge until you find the temperature zone that holds the most walleyes.

Fishing During the Spawning Season

Anglers frequently debate the ethics of catching walleyes during the spawning season. Some maintain that the practice is not sporting and that taking walleyes at spawning time will damage future fishing. But others say fishing at spawning time is no different than fishing in late fall. In fact, the big females are more vulnerable in late fall because they are feeding heavily to nourish their eggs.

Most waters in the northern states and Canada are closed to walleye fishing around spawning time. Portions of the Great Lakes, some rivers and reservoirs in the North and most waters in the South are open continuously.

The spawning period offers some of the year's best fishing, and some of the worst. If the weather stays warm for a few days, walleyes usually bite well. A rise in water temperature of only a degree or two can trigger a burst of feeding. But a cold front, even if it is not severe, has the opposite effect.

As a rule, walleyes bite better in the afternoon than in the morning, especially early in the spawning season. If the water temperature rises gradually through the day, as it often does, fishing peaks at about 3 or 4 P.M.

In rivers, fishing during the spawning period is best in years when the water level is low and stable. Walleyes concentrate in pools and eddies, so they are easy to find. In high water, they scatter into flooded vegetation where finding and catching them is difficult.

When and where walleyes spawn depends on latitude (p. 169) and type of water. For details pertaining to the type of water you fish, refer to the section, "Where to Find Walleyes through the Seasons" (page 64).

How to Catch Pre-Spawn Walleyes

In the early stages of the spawning period, you can usually find walleyes in deep water in the vicinity of their spawning area. In most cases, they will be at depths of 15 to 30 feet.

Because the water temperature is cold, walleyes are not feeding aggressively. You can often catch them by jigging vertically with a jig and minnow, or a vibrating blade. Vertical jigging will usually take more fish than casting and retrieving because you can feel the subtle strikes more easily. If you are missing too many fish, attach a stinger hook to your jig.

Later in the pre-spawn period, walleyes begin to feed more actively. They mill about near the spawning area, sometimes moving into water only 2 to 3 feet deep, even during the day. Anglers often make the mistake of fishing too deep, especially if the water is discolored from runoff.

A jig still works well, but because the fish are more aggressive, you may not have to tip it with a minnow. If you can get by without one, you will probably miss fewer short strikers. Another effective technique is casting or long-line trolling with a shallow-running crankbait or minnow plug. You can also use a small minnow on a split-shot rig.

FISHING TIPS FOR THE EARLY PRE-SPAWN PERIOD

•*Jig vertically* with a 1/4- to 3/8-ounce jig, using a gentle up-and-down motion. Or simply swim it close to bottom, with little jigging action. Avoid bouncing the jig high off bottom with long sweeps of the rod.

•*Tighten* your line slowly when you feel a slight nudge or the jig seems a little heavier than normal. Walleyes often grab the tail of the minnow, so it pays to hesitate a moment before setting the hook.

FISHING TIPS FOR THE LATE PRE-SPAWN PERIOD

•*Slow-troll* a minnow plug along a riprap, bank, rocky shoreline or shallow spawning shoal at dusk or just after dark. Let out at least 100 feet of line and, if possible, use a quiet electric motor to propel the boat.

•*Quietly anchor* near a spawning shoal, but keep your boat far enough away to prevent spooking the fish. Fan-cast the shoal using a 1/16- to 1/8-ounce jig. Keep repositioning your boat until you locate the fish.

How to Catch Walleyes at Spawning Time

Timing is the most important consideration for anglers who fish at spawning time. Although females will not bite once they start to spawn, all of them do not spawn at the same time. Those that have not started to spawn can still be caught. But as the spawning period progresses, fishing for females becomes a waste of time.

In years when the water warms slowly, however, females that spawned early resume feeding before the spawning period is over. Fishing gradually picks up as more females recover.

When females are in the midst of spawning, you can find others that have not started to spawn by moving to a body of water where the timing of the spawning run is different. Or you can work different spawning areas in the same body of water. In some lakes, for instance, one segment of the population spawns in a tributary stream, another along the shoreline and yet another on an offshore reef. Stream spawning begins first; shoreline spawning a week or more later; and reef spawning another week or more after shoreline spawning. So even if the stream fish are in the middle of spawning, many of the reef fish have not started to spawn.

QUICK TIP: Male walleyes continue to bite even though spawning has begun. You can catch them in water only a few feet deep. After spawning has been in progress for several days, almost all of the fish caught are males.

APPROXIMATE DATE OF SPAWNING PEAK AT DIFFERENT LATITUDES

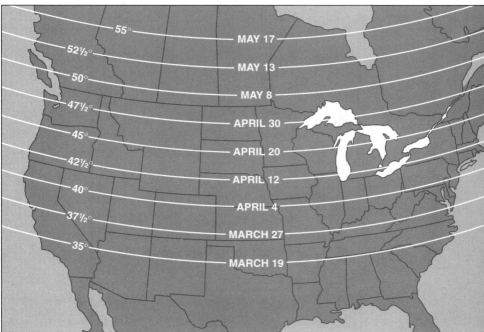

SPAWNING begins much earlier in the South than in the North. In waters at a latitude of 35°N, walleye spawning activity peaks on March 19 in a typical year. But at a latitude of 55°N, the spawning peak is not until May 17. At a given latitude, the peak may be a week earlier in shallow bodies of water; a week later in deep ones. And, the peak may be 10 days sooner in an early spring; 10 days later in a late one.

The techniques used to catch walleyes at spawning time are much the same as those used in the late pre-spawn period.

How to Catch Post-Spawn Walleyes

By the time walleyes recover from spawning, the water temperature is warm enough that they feed much more aggressively than they did a few weeks earlier. But finding them may not be easy.

Some males remain in the spawning area, but most walleyes work their way toward their summer locations, feeding on shallow points, breaklines and reefs close to shore. During

the day, they normally hold at depths of 15 feet or less. You can locate them by trolling with a crankbait or minnow plug or with a slip-sinker rig baited with a minnow, leech or night-crawler. If you find a school, anchor your boat and cast with a plain or tipped jig, a minnow on a split-shot rig, or a weight-forward spinner.

If the weather stays cool into the post-spawn period, walleyes will not begin feeding as early as they normally would. If you locate fish but they seem reluctant to bite, try a slip-bobber rig baited with a leech or minnow. Under these conditions, a bait that is not moving may be the secret.

In the evening, walleyes may move in as shallow as 2 feet, especially if sunny, calm weather has warmed the shallows. You can locate them by shining the feeding shoals with a spotlight. When you see glowing eyes, turn off the light. Shining spooks the fish, but you can return an hour or so later and catch them with a floating minnow plug.

TECHNIQUES FOR POST-SPAWN WALLEYES

•*Anchor* your boat upstream from a current-brushed point in a big river. Cast a 1/4- to 3/8-ounce jig downstream of the point, then retrieve with slow hops. Walleyes usually hold in moving water off the tip.

•*Work* stump fields along old creek channels using a pony-head jig tipped with a nightcrawler, or a crankbait. Reservoir walleyes often move into stump fields after spawning, sometimes into water only 5 feet deep.

•*Cast* a floating minnow plug over a feeding shoal beginning at dusk. Some fishermen work the shoals by wading; others prefer to slip along silently using an electric motor while casting into the shallows.

Cold Fronts

The toughest time to catch walleyes is after a severe cold front. Normally, crisp temperatures and ultra-clear skies follow passage of the front. Walleyes respond by tightly hugging the bottom or burying themselves in dense weedbeds. They feed sporadically if at all. Depending on the severity of the cold front, it may take up to 3 days for the fish to resume normal activity.

Post-cold front conditions present problems for even the best fishermen, but the following tactics may improve your success:

•*Do your fishing* very early or very late in the day, or at night. Your odds of finding active walleyes are best during low-light periods. In early spring, however, they may bite better during the warmest part of the day. Feeding periods following a cold front are likely to be short.

•*Fish 5 to 10 feet deeper* than you normally would at a given time of day. Increased light penetration from the clear skies drives the walleyes into deeper, darker water.

•*Try fishing* in the weeds. Some walleyes will seek cover in shallow vegetation rather than move to

COLD-FRONT conditions cause walleyes to lie on bottom in a state of near-dormancy. Normally walleyes are extremely shy of divers, but after a cold front, a diver can often swim up to a walleye and touch it. The increased light penetration causes a reaction called dazzlement, or partial blindness due to bright light.

deep structure. Weed walleyes resume normal activity before the walleyes in deeper water.

•*Use live bait.* A small bait will usually work better than a large one. Walleyes in a lethargic state are not likely to chase a fast-moving artificial.

•*Fish slowly.* Walleyes may even ignore live bait if it is moving too fast. Anchoring is often more effective than trolling or drifting.

•*Attach a stinger hook* if the fish are striking short. A half-interested walleye will often take a nip at the tail of a minnow or crawler, then let go before you can set the hook. With a stinger, you will hook a good percentage of these fish.

•*Use light, clear line.* Post-cold front walleyes are particularly line-shy. Some fishermen use monofilament as light as 4-pound test.

•*If you are fishing* on a relatively clear lake with no success, try a lake with darker water or a river.

•*In large, shallow lakes* with silty bottoms, the strong winds accompanying a cold front stir up the bottom. For several days after the front, the water may be so turbid that you have to fish shallower than normal if the walleyes are to see your bait. In most cases, midday fishing is best.

TIPS FOR FISHING UNDER COLD-FRONT CONDITIONS

•*Dangle* a minnow or leech from a lighted slip-bobber starting at dusk. A stationary bait may tempt inactive walleyes to bite, and you can easily see the bobber.

•*Tie* a slip-sinker rig using a leader no more than 18 inches long. A lethargic walleye will not swim upward to grab your bait; a short leader keeps your bait near bottom.

•*Use* a lighter-than-normal jig, and tip it with live bait. A lighter jig takes more time to sink, so it forces you to retrieve very slowly and gives the fish extra time to strike.

Ultra-Clear Water

Anglers who live on ultra-clear walleye lakes often complain that the waters are fished out. But when they voice these complaints to conservation agencies, they often learn that good numbers of walleyes were caught in test nets.

Walleyes in ultra-clear lakes, where the clarity is 10 feet or more, are much harder to catch than those in low-clarity waters. The fish may feed at depths of 5 feet or less at night, then retreat to water over 40 feet deep in midday. And in water this clear, they are easily spooked by any unusual sound or sudden movement.

On calm, sunny days, walleyes in these waters feed most heavily around dusk and dawn, or at night. On windy or overcast days, they also feed at dusk and dawn, but some feeding takes place during midday.

The secret to catching walleyes in clear lakes is to keep noise and movement to an absolute minimum, especially when fishing in water less than 20 feet deep. You can often double or triple the number of strikes by using 4-pound-test line instead of 8-pound test. Use clear or low-visibility line instead of fluorescent line.

To prevent spooking the walleyes, keep your boat as far from the fishing area as possible. Anchor and use long casts to reach the fish instead of hovering in place and fishing vertically. When trolling in shallow water, use a light sinker. This forces you to let out a lot of line in order to reach bottom. If possible, use an electric trolling motor instead of your outboard.

When fishing with live-bait rigs in ultra-clear water, it usually pays to use a plain hook and as little hardware as possible. Most anglers prefer a slip-sinker, split-shot or slip-bobber rig. By still-fishing with a slip-bobber, you can avoid continually casting or trolling over the walleyes.

The best artificials are those with a natural look. Dark colors generally work better than bright or fluorescent colors. Minnow plugs outperform crankbaits because they more closely resemble the baitfish prevalent in these waters. Black-and-silver, black-and-gold, and perch finishes work best. Jigs also produce well, especially when tipped with a minnow. Black, purple and brown jigs are usually most effective.

In the clearest lakes, you may have no choice but to fish at night, especially during periods of sunny weather. Use the same baits, lures and techniques that you would during the day, but fish in much shallower water. Some fishermen prefer wading to fishing from a boat because they can move quietly along the shore without spooking the walleyes.

Clear lakes usually have lush growths of submerged weeds. And the weeds grow in much deeper water than in other lakes. If the weeds are dense, you may find walleyes in relatively shallow water, even if the weather is sunny. Or they may move deeper and hold in the area where weed density tapers off. Anyone who spends much time fishing in clear lakes should become familiar with the techniques for catching walleyes in weeds.

TIPS FOR FISHING IN ULTRA-CLEAR WATER

•*Add* a flicker (size 00) blade to your live-bait rig. The small blade has enough flash to draw a walleye's attention in clear water. A larger blade would look unnatural.

•*Rig* your line on a planer board when trolling in the shallows of a clear lake. Let out 50 to 100 feet of line, attach it to the board, then let out more line. The board will pull your line as much as 50 feet to the side of the boat's wake so you do not spook the fish. With a breakaway-style board, a strike frees the line so you can fight the fish without interference from the board.

•*Avoid* racing up to your fishing spot. The commotion will scare the fish. Instead, cut the engine at least 100 feet from the spot, then move in with your electric motor.

Low-Clarity Water

Most walleye fishermen would be surprised to learn that low-clarity waters frequently support more walleyes than clear waters. Low-clarity waters are usually high in the nutrients needed for a healthy food chain. And because low-clarity waters filter out sunlight, walleyes can spend more time in the food-rich shallows.

Low-clarity water usually results from one or more of the following:

•Suspended mud or clay resulting from carp, bullheads or other rough fish stirring up the bottom, from wave action in a shallow basin, or from erosion of nearby farmlands.

•A heavy algae bloom caused by highly fertile water. The water may be very clear in spring and fall, but greenish or brownish in summer.

•Bog stain caused by decomposition of tree leaves and aquatic vegetation.

Walleye fishing in low-clarity waters tends to be more consistent than in clear waters. The fish seem less affected by weather changes, particularly cold fronts. Because the walleyes stay relatively shallow most of the time, they are easier to find.

> QUICK TIP: Avoid fishing in waters where you can see clouds of rolling mud. This condition often exists after a torrential rain, especially in rivers and reservoirs. With the turbidity level this high, walleyes have a difficult time zeroing in on any kind of lure or bait.

Your fishing strategy in these waters depends on the visibility. If it is less than a foot, artificial lures usually work better than live bait. It is easier for walleyes to detect the sound, vibration and brighter color of an artificial. If you prefer live bait, add a fluorescent spinner or other colorful attractor.

Walleyes in waters where visibility is less than a foot generally bite best in midday. Fishing from 10 A.M. to 4 P.M. is usually better than at dawn or dusk. Night fishing is likely to be poor. Calm, sunny days are better than cloudy, windy days.

The best lures for these waters usually produce sound or vibration. Crankbaits and vibrating plugs with rattle chambers, vibrating blades, and spinners are good choices. Surprisingly, jigs work well even though they produce comparatively little vibration. Untipped jigs are just as effective as jigs tipped with live bait. Walleyes in low-clarity waters are conditioned to strike at any glimpse of movement or anytime they detect vibration with their lateral-line system. Live bait does not add to the visibility or vibration and may result in short strikes.

If the visibility is from one to three feet, live bait is probably a better all-around choice than artificial lures. But a spinner or other attractor on your live-bait rig will produce more fish.

Fishing in morning and late afternoon is usually better than fishing at midday, but the walleyes will start biting later and stop earlier than in clearer water. Cloudy or windy days are usually better than calm, sunny days. If the visibility exceeds 3 feet, strategies for low-clarity water are not needed.

LURES FOR LOW-CLARITY WATER

•*Fluorescent lures* are more visible to walleyes in low-clarity water than non-fluorescent lures. Fluorescent colors have a higher luminance, meaning that they reflect more light. If an object reflects 100 percent of the light, its luminance is 1; if it reflects no light, its luminance is 0. Some fluorescent colors have a luminance value over 1; they actually emit more light than they receive. Of the fluorescent colors, orange is most visible in low-clarity water, followed by red and yellow. Of the non-fluorescent colors, white, orange and red are most visible.

•*Phosphorescent lures*, or "glow-in-the-dark" lures, produce a soft glow that is visible to walleyes in low-clarity water or during low-light conditions in clear water. You can buy crankbaits and jig heads coated with phosphorescent paint and soft-plastic tails with phosphorescence molded in. Phosphorescent lures must be recharged about once every 10 minutes to maintain their glow. Simply expose them to any source of bright light. Some fishermen believe that phosphorescent lures work better after the peak glow subsides. If they glow too brightly, they may spook the walleyes.

Trophy Walleyes

A walleye over 10 pounds ranks among the greatest prizes in freshwater fishing. Catching a walleye that size is a difficult and often frustrating task, even for an accomplished angler.

Few bodies of water contain large numbers of big walleyes. In a moderately fished lake, for instance, the combination of natural mortality and angling catch reduces the number of fish of a given age by about 50 percent each year. Thus, if a population contained 1,000 1-year-old walleyes, 500 would remain at age 2, 250 at age 3, and only 2 at age 10.

Adding to the challenge is the fact that big walleyes are much warier than small ones. Their exceedingly cautious nature explains why they live so long. If a big walleye sees or hears anything unusual, it stops feeding and heads for deeper water. Trophy hunters know that the poorest time to catch a big walleye is on the weekend when the lake is overrun with water skiers and pleasure boaters.

If you fish long enough, you may catch a trophy walleye using the same strategy you would employ for average-sized walleyes. But you can greatly boost your odds by selecting waters likely to produce big fish, carefully choosing your fishing times and using techniques suited to trophy walleyes.

SELECTING THE WATER. One of the best-kept secrets in fishing is the location of a spot that produces trophy walleyes. It is highly unlikely that a fisherman who specializes in big walleyes will tell you where he catches his fish.

Many types of water are capable of producing big walleyes. You may find your trophy in a deep oligotrophic lake or in a shallow eutrophic lake infested with rough fish. In general, rivers are poorer choices than natural lakes or reservoirs because the fish grow more slowly. But large rivers impounded by dams produce some of the finest trophy-walleye fishing to be found anywhere.

In recent years, much has been written about trophy-walleye fishing in the Southeast. Reservoirs in this area produce some giant walleyes because of the fast growth rate (page 40). But walleyes in the North are more abundant and have a much longer life span. Even though the top-end weights are not quite as high, northern waters produce many more walleyes of 10 pounds or more.

If you want to catch a big walleye, but do not know where to go, base your choice on the following:

• *Water area* – All other factors being equal, a large body of water is more likely to support big walleyes than a small one. A 500-acre natural lake may hold a few 10-pound walleyes, but on a per-acre basis, a 5000-acre lake would hold a lot more.

•*Size of walleye population* – Waters that produce lots of small walleyes generally yield few trophies. Competition for food and living space makes it more difficult for the fish to grow to a large size. Strange as it may sound, your chances of boating a big walleye are often better in a body of water not known for good walleye fishing.

Waters where walleyes are plentiful usually attract large numbers of anglers. Heavy fishing pressure reduces the average size of the walleyes and cuts your odds of boating a trophy.

•*Usable forage* – A body of water may be full of forage fish, but if they are not of a size acceptable to walleyes, they do not contribute to the trophy potential. In fact, a large population of unusable forage is detrimental. The productivity of any body of water is limited, so the larger the population of oversized forage, the smaller the crop of usable forage.

For example, many lakes in the North contain large populations of ciscoes. But in most cases, the cisco crop consists mainly of fish over 10 inches in length, too big for the vast majority of walleyes. These lakes produce few trophies. A few northern lakes, however, have populations of dwarf ciscoes, a strain that never grows longer than 7 inches. These lakes have much greater potential for big walleyes.

WHEN TO CATCH TROPHY WALLEYES. Anglers catch by far the most trophy walleyes during the following three periods: just before spawning; in early summer, when the big females have completely recuperated from spawning; and in late fall, when the fish are feeding heavily in preparation for winter.

During the pre-spawn period, large numbers of big females crowd into a relatively small area. Although they are not feeding heavily, you may be able to catch a fish or two because of the sheer numbers present. Good fishing lasts until spawning begins.

About 2 weeks after spawning, the big females start to bite again, but they are still scattered and can be very difficult to find. You may catch an occasional large walleye, but seldom more than one. Your chances of finding a concentration of big walleyes are much better after they have settled into their typical summer locations. The best fishing begins about 5 to 6 weeks after spawning and generally lasts 2 to 3 weeks.

Late-fall fishing is extremely unpredictable, but if you can find the walleyes, a high percentage of them will be big. The preponderance of large walleyes in late fall can be explained by the fact that most of them are females. To nourish their developing eggs, females must consume more food than males, up to six times more according to some feeding studies.

In waters that stratify, the depths are warmer than the shallows once the fall turnover is completed. Big walleyes may swim into shallow water for short feeding sprees, but at other times may be found as deep as 50 feet. Although difficult to find, they form tight schools, so you may be able to catch several from the same area.

TECHNIQUES FOR TROPHY WALLEYES. Catching a walleye over 10 pounds is a once-in-a-lifetime accomplishment for most anglers. But some fishermen catch several that size each year. If you spend a lot of time fishing waters known for trophy walleyes, but seldom land a big one, you are probably making one or more of the following mistakes:

•You may be fishing at the wrong depth. In most waters, big walleyes feed in the shallows during low-light periods, especially in spring and fall. But at most other times, they prefer relatively deep water, deeper than the areas where you typically find smaller walleyes.

Often, big walleyes use the same structure as the smaller ones, but hang 10 to 15 feet deeper. This behavior can be attributed to a walleye's increasing sensitivity to light as it grows older. In addition, bigger walleyes prefer cooler water, and they can usually find it by moving deeper.

In deep northern lakes, however, the shallow water stays cool enough for big walleyes through the summer. If the walleyes can find boulders or other shallow-water cover to provide shade, they may spend the summer at depths of 10 feet or less. In these lakes, most anglers fish too deep.

•You may be using baits and lures too small to interest trophy walleyes. If you have ever cleaned a big walleye, you were probably surprised to find one or more 6- to 8-inch baitfish in its stomach. Yet few walleye anglers would consider tying on a bait this large. Instead, they use smaller baits and, not surprisingly, catch smaller walleyes.

Big baits draw far fewer strikes than small ones, and most anglers are not willing to fish all day for one or two opportunities. But if you are intent on catching a trophy, that is the price you must pay.

•You may be fishing at the wrong time of day. If the water is very clear, or if there is a great deal of boat traffic, big walleyes will feed almost exclusively at night.

•Your presentation may be too sloppy. Many fishermen assume that they need big hooks and heavy leaders to catch trophy walleyes, but the reverse is actually true. Big walleyes are extremely cautious. They are much more likely to take a bait attached to a size 6 hook and a 6-pound-test leader than one attached to a 1/0 hook and 15-pound leader. In clear water, some trophy specialists use a 4-pound leader.

A small hook allows a walleye to swallow the bait without feeling anything unusual. And a small hook will not break or pull out. Most big walleyes are hooked under snag-free conditions, so if you take your time and do not attempt to horse the fish, light line will do the job.

Another common mistake is making too much noise. Unless the fish are in water deeper than 20 feet, you should not troll over them with your outboard motor. Avoid dropping anything in the boat and do not attempt to anchor on top of the fish. Set your anchor at a distance and let the wind drift your boat into position.

TIPS FOR CATCHING TROPHY WALLEYES

•*Check* your line frequently, especially when fishing for trophy walleyes. You may get only a few bites each day, so you do not want to lose a fish because of a frayed line.

•*Use* minnow plugs up to 8 inches long. Big lures work better than small lures; a big walleye can save energy by eating one large baitfish instead of several smaller ones.

•*Select* a jig with a hook larger than normal (right, top) when tipping with big minnows. A smaller one (right, bottom) will hook fewer fish because too little of the hook is exposed.

TIPS ON NIGHT FISHING FOR TROPHY WALLEYES

•*Scout* likely walleye structure during midday, when fishing is slow. Anchor a large white jug on the edge of a shallow reef or shoal likely to hold walleyes at night. Remember the position of the jug so that you can find the exact spot after dark.

•*Locate* the jug with a spotlight, but avoid shining the beam into the water because it may spook the fish. When you spot the jug, shut off your outboard. Let the breeze push you into position or move in with an electric motor. Anchor upwind of the spot you want to fish.

Putting It All Together

Let's make the following assumptions:

•You have selected productive walleye water, and will be there at the right time of year.

•You have the proper equipment for the situation.

•You understand a walleye's food and habitat preferences and how it reacts to environmental changes such as weather and light intensity.

Now, your major challenge is to locate the fish and find a presentation that will make them bite.

Discovering the right combination of location and presentation is called finding the pattern. The ability to find the pattern quickly is what separates the expert from the average walleye fisherman.

The first step in finding the pattern is to use your knowledge of walleye behavior and seasonal movements to make an educated guess at where the fish will be. Examine a lake map and identify the most likely areas. Then, choose a presentation suited to the habitat and the mood of the walleyes. Take into account the type of water, time of year, cloud cover, wind speed and direction, and time of day.

If the pattern you choose does not pay off in a half hour or so, analyze all the available information, then try something different. For example, if you are marking walleyes on your flasher or graph, but cannot make them bite, it makes little sense to move to another spot. Instead, try a different bait or troll at a slightly slower speed. Or try adding a spinner or other attractor to trigger the fish. Often, a minor change in presentation makes a big difference.

To better understand the principles of finding the pattern, consider how an experienced walleye fisherman would handle this hypothetical situation:

The body of water is a typical mesotrophic walleye lake with water clarity of about 8 feet. It is early in the season and the walleyes completed spawning only a week ago. The skies are overcast and there is a breeze from the southeast.

Checking his lake map, the angler finds two gradually sloping points along the northwest shore. One is about 1/4 mile from a spawning creek, the other about 3/4 mile. Both appear to be likely spots, considering the season and the wind direction.

After motoring to the point closest to the creek, he checks the structure with his flasher. But the signal is weak, indicating a mucky bottom. Without wasting time fishing this unlikely spot, he motors to the other point. This one looks much better; the flasher shows a double echo. A few bulrushes are beginning to poke out of the water on the shallow portion of the point, indicating a firm, sandy bottom.

Taking into account the cold water and the likelihood of walleyes being scattered at this time of year, he decides to troll around the point using a shiner minnow on a slip-sinker rig. Starting his trolling run at 8 feet, he works his way out to 15 feet, then back in again. On the second pass around the point, he feels a light pick-up at 12 feet, but the fish drops the bait. Several more passes result in one more pickup, but again the fish does not hold on.

Reasoning that there is a school of walleye holding on the point but not actively feeding, he decides to try a slower presentation. He anchors the boat far enough off the point that he will not spook the fish, but can still reach them. He rigs up a slip-bobber, hooks on a leech, sets the depth at 11 feet, then casts to the precise spot where the fish bit.

Almost immediately, the bobber goes under. He sets the hook and reels in a 2-pound walleye. In only 45 minutes, he has his limit, including one spawned-out female weighing 8 pounds.

If the fisherman had not understood the elements discussed earlier, he would have gone home empty-handed. For example, without an understanding of seasonal movement patterns and the effects of weather, he would never have found the spot in the first place. Without a sensitive rod, he would not have felt the light pick-ups that told him that fish were present. And without the versatility to try a different presentation, he might have struggled for a fish or two, but probably no more.

INDEX

Vertical jigging, 115-117, 123, 148, 162, 163, 167, 168
When to use, 135, 139, 141, 142, 162, 173, 175, 178, 184
Jig Trolling, 117, 162

L

Lakes, 60-62
  Boats & motors, 12-13
  See also: Eutrophic Lakes, Mesotrophic Lakes, Oligotrophic Lakes, Reservoirs
Lateral-Line Sense, 33, 123
Leaders, 105, 110
Leeches, 37, 102
  Keeping alive, 113
  Rigs & hooking, 105, 106, 109, 112, 120, 136, 147, 149, 171, 173
Length of Walleyes at Various Ages (chart), 40-41
Light Levels, 50-52, 54, 56
  And walleye seasonal locations, 64-66
Line, 10, 11, 184
  For leaders, 105, 110
  For planer-board fishing, 150
  For snaggy bottoms, 142
  Line weight & reel selection, 9
Liquid-Crystal Recorders, 14, 17
  See also: Depth Finders
Live Bait,
  Fishing techniques, 102-113, 135, 164, 165, 173, 175, 176, 178
  Keeping bait alive, 25, 113
  Rods & reels, 8, 9
Log Jams, 78
Low-Clarity Water, 43, 72, 75, 177-179
  And line selection, 11
  And moon phase, 58
  And walleye coloration, 30
  Baits, lures & techniques, 108, 110, 115, 117, 123, 125
  Effects of light levels, 51, 54

M

Markers, 24
Mesotrophic Lakes, 36, 60-61, 66-68, 134
Mice, 37
Minnow Plugs, 124-125, 137, 139, 148, 163, 167, 168, 171, 175, 184
Minnows, 102
  Keeping alive, 25, 113
  Rigs & hooking, 105, 106, 109, 112,

115, 120, 136, 137, 139, 147, 162, 167, 171, 173, 175
Moon Phase, 57-59
Motors, see: Boats & Motors
Mud Flats, 75
Mudpuppies, 37
Murky Water, see: Low-Clarity Water

N

Natural Lakes, see: Lakes
Nightcrawlers, 102
  Inflating, 140, 149
  Keeping alive, 113
  Rigs & hooking, 105, 106, 109, 112, 120, 121, 128, 136, 139, 140, 142, 147, 149, 171
Night Fishing, 108, 110, 168, 172, 175, 184, 185

O

Oligotrophic Lakes, 62, 66, 68-70, 134
Outboards, see: Boats & Motors
Overcast Weather, 50, 52, 53, 56, 69, 175
Oxygen Levels in Water, 44, 72, 87
  And walleye locations, 65, 72, 75, 134, 144

P

pH of Water, 45
Phosphorescent Lures, 179
Pike-Perch, 31
Planer Boards, 150-153, 176
  Diving planers, 154, 156-157
Plankton, 65, 72
Plugs, 123-127, 163, 171
  See also: Crankbaits, Minnow Plugs, Vibrating Plugs
Points, 88, 93, 94, 171
  Walleye locations, 53, 67, 68, 69, 71, 73-75, 77, 78
Pools in Rivers, 78, 162-165, 167
Population Data, 88
Propellers, 15

R

Rainy Weather, 53
Range of Walleyes, 28-29
Rapids, 73, 78
Redtail Chubs, 102
Reefs & Humps, 88, 89, 93, 94
  Lures & techniques, 116
  Walleye locations, 53, 68-70, 72, 74, 77, 144
Reels, see: Rods & Reels

Creative Publishing international, Inc. offers a variety of how-to books. For information write:
  Creative Publishing international, Inc.
  Subscriber Books
  5900 Green Oak Drive
  Minnetonka, MN 55343